# S UNFORGIVABLE
# IN

*Blaspheme Against The Holy Spirit -*
*A Holy Spirit Inspired Teaching*

## QUAIL-CHILD

WESTBOW
PRESS®
A DIVISION OF THOMAS NELSON
& ZONDERVAN

WestBow Press books may be ordered through booksellers or by contacting:

WestBow Press
A Division of Thomas Nelson & Zondervan
1663 Liberty Drive
Bloomington, IN 47403
www.westbowpress.com
844-714-3454

ISBN: 978-1-6642-9681-7 (sc)
ISBN: 978-1-6642-9683-1 (hc)
ISBN: 978-1-6642-9682-4 (e)

Library of Congress Control Number: 2023906401

Print information available on the last page.

WestBow Press rev. date: 05/16/2023

# CONTENTS

Hello,

I greet you in the name of Jesus, my Lord and Savior, and pray my story provide insight and hope for you. In His Mighty name, amen.

My name is Apostle Quail-Child, and I am excited to share a piece of my life with you in hopes it inspires you as the Word of God says: "They triumphed over him by the blood of the Lamb and by the word of their testimony; they did not love their lives so much as to shrink from death" (New International Version, Revelation 12.11). Therefore, my faith says that as I boldly share my testimony, which is now mixed with the precious blood of the Lamb, I have power to defeat evil – this should encourage us all!

I was saved in the summer of 2012 with my family in Victory Outreach Church, Phoenix AZ, after thirteen years of marriage. Just months prior to this time, my family and I had lived in Charlotte NC, but we had moved back to AZ following a severe neck injury I sustained – where my cervical seven in my neck was broken along with several other fractured bones in my neck. Glory to God I went into the hospital paralyzed and walked out of the hospital the next day with a neck brace. This was after much discussion among the doctors who were considering a full body cast at one point during my short hospital stay.

Although now this miracle seems great hearing this, and it is, but at that time this ended up becoming the entry point of the enemy who then wreaked havoc upon me, my wife and children and many other loved ones. I was prescribed a narcotic drug for nerve pain as my spinal cord had been severely bruised – to this day I suffer itchiness in my neck area between my shoulder blades and along both sides of my upper side arms, and tingly and numbness in my index fingers and thumbs. The pain medication ended up making me very manic – my brother in-law living with us at the time, who previously was a meth-addict, once told me: "You remind me of myself when I was cracked-out". While on this medication I often had moments of hallucinations – where in my mind I saw dead people … some I once knew, but others like Bob Marley I didn't … I felt I knew them in those moments. Sounds so ridiculous I know, but this was a demonic stronghold I was totally unaware of and totally unprepared for.

With the neck brace on and with my Dr's instructions to be extremely careful, I was adamant to start my own business, and had started talks with friends and potential clients in the aerospace manufacturing industry, about potential manufacturing opportunities where I would partner with previous employers and customers in Phoenix AZ, Chino CA and Torrance CA. Shortly after returning from a quick trip to AZ for these discussions, I ended up losing contact with all my prospects, and fell into deep depression. After a long spell of depression, I started to regain my sanity and confidence. Now, to add some context leading up to this point: the prior three years I had gone back to school to complete my business management degree, while taking care of my youngest son who had been diagnosed with childhood adrenoleukodystrophy (ALD) in October 2008. My son's diagnosis was the motivation to move out of AZ away from family, and to deal and cope with this mortifying season privately.

Fast forward three years later with my neck injury, I then found a job back in Phoenix AZ and again all chaos broke loose ... With my neck still healing, my wife at the time was parting ways with her employer who had blessed us three years prior with an amazing relocation package and an awesome job-advancement for her and our family. By the time she made it back to AZ in a rush, driving our children home and with all our belongings in a large U-Haul truck, she came back to find out I had been jailed for the first time in my life. Here I am at the age of thirty-five − never had any prior run ins with the law, other than for minor things in my pre-teens and a few speeding tickets throughout the years. Everyone was besides themselves − "Not the Quail-Child I know," they would say ... oh yes, me. I had at this point allowed and invited the enemy in. My wife will tell you I had the blackest eyes of evil − I was made lukewarm without knowing what it was spiritually − the mixture of evil and good. I was so lost − thinking I could toggle between the devil and God. Ridiculous me! Brings disgusting chills over my body even now writing about this.

Then I was institutionalized in a mental ward for some time – court ordered. This really fueled my anger, regretfully, even hatred towards my family at the time (namely my father, mom and wife). I was diagnosed with bipolar disorder. Upon my release of the mental institution, I became even more lost … I hate to admit this, but I cannot take away from my testimony, nor exaggerate it – in 2011, I landed a male stripper job and worked it for months that fall and early winter.

About this time, and certainly by the grace of God, out of nowhere I started becoming depressed again, and even contrite. As the Lord would prepare me, unbeknownst to me, my dad would invite me and my wife to church – where he had been going faithfully for several years. My wife who was waiting to be served with divorce papers, told me: "In order to see your kids, you need to come to church with us". I agreed … that following Sunday a seed was planted in my heart – deep conviction of all my recent wrong doings fell strongly upon my conscience. However, I would leave my family again … struggling with my promiscuity and the convicting words the Lord used through the preacher-man. This was my battle … yet I would continuously give in to my flesh … my selfish desires.

The seed of truth and contrition started to light my conscience on fire! In my secret place, I found myself crying out to God – far away from my family and those who loved me. It was a cold place, desolate, empty, a deep pit of Hades where no love was felt. Then, Lord of Mercy and Grace consumed me with His loving fire, reigniting me with hope. From there His grace stuck with me, and the good fight began. Quickly was reconciled back to my family, my job in the aerospace industry was restored, church became our Sunday joy as a family and my wife and I were on a slow but encouraging road to marital recovery knowing Jesus was now on our side relationally as one flesh under His Lordship. Shortly afterwards, we bought our next house … no more living with other family members … no more rentals … we no longer needed governmental assistance for basic living needs … we, yet again, had our own place we could call home with God supplying all our needs.

My wife became a member of the church choir after a year's time. Me, well … I was still a convicted mess at the altar. God had me broken for two years – immersed in contrition. I was over the feeling of guilt and self-condemnation for I knew I was washed in His blood and set free in forgiveness, but I felt so bad and disappointed in myself for the errors of my past ways. Right around the first year of being in the church, my dad bought me and my wife our first study Bibles. Next-level spiritual growth and maturity would soon ensue on our family's behalf.

Then God would start to clearly speak to me. My first charge by Him in spirit: "Son, read Me from the beginning to the end". As I would read the Bible starting in the Old Testament, He began to engulf my conscience in spirit – bringing His word alive. I often refer to this experience having been similar when I watched the movie, *The Never-Ending Story*, as a child for the first time – but my read of the Bible as an adult would be even more real and alive supernaturally … which continues to this day. Ever since, I am addicted to the Bible.

Ministry outside our family's home started to develop quickly after the second year in the church. My wife remained faithful serving on the choir, and I received my first pre-calling apart from our family ministry in our own home … it was with the men's recovery home with our church – to preach, teach and counsel the Word of God with the men in the recovery program. This ministry first started as once a month, then progressed to once every week. While my wife was at choir practice on Thursdays, I was preaching and teaching at the recovery home. We still serve in this ministry when we can to this day – our first family's ministry together outside our home.

A couple years after serving in the recovery home, and in parallel with that service, I received the second pre-calling. This calling was to minister to the homeless men and women in the downtown Phoenix area. We served in this ministry alongside another faithful lighthouse our family partnered with in the area, which was Urban

Outreach Church under the Assemblies of God – a part of the largest Pentecostal denomination. This was a fruitful experience!

Then the ultimate calling came to me after serving in the ministry four years. I say 'ultimate' carefully, knowing that my fallible knowledge as to the future is real, and truly only God knows the entirety of what's in store for me and my family in serving Him. That said, after returning from a Tennessee trip in the spring of 2018, where God ministered to me at a youth revival (Warrior Fest) in the city of Ooltewah with the Perry Stone and Eddie James ministries at the Omega Center International campus. This was a remarkable experience! On the way home we were driving through Gallup NM, the call came during my third baptism with Holy Spirit while I was driving. Mind you, my whole family was asleep in the van during this encounter. The Lord spoke to me: "Son, you will pastor the love, hope and trust of My Son Jesus Christ with a primary focus upon Indigenous lands of North America". This moment was a flurry of spiritual fireworks all around me – crying, free flowing snot from my nose, laughter, speaking in tongues, singing with joy, seeing visions of God's glory … it was an amazing moment that set my spirit ablaze to the very core – an unquenchable fire-conviction to engage with loving action. Nothing was satisfying to me during this time unless I was working towards His calling over my life.

After a good week's praying upon our return, we were led out of the church we were first attending. We were then led to a Vietnamese church in Mesa AZ, where I would help pastor the youth. The church also put me through ministerial schooling through the International School of Ministry (ISOM) and funded all of it. By God's grace, I completed the one-year degree program in six months. I am now a legally ordained minister … but more importantly I am a spiritually ordained servant of The Most-High God. The paper helps to win the hearts of the World with a great chance to salvation, but God's ordination has the invisible and divine power to perpetuate His will through my yielded vessel. Paper and titles don't cast devils out of the souls of God's children … it is only by His Spirit of Grace. Halleluiah!

As of April 2018, our family is a fully 501(c)3 non-profit organization under the name, *Living on the Rock Ministries*, where the calling, vision and mission are established and protected under the Lordship of Christ according to the Father's will. We operate this while I work a secular job in the aerospace industry. God is good … as it is written: "Every good and perfect gift is from above, coming down from the Father of the heavenly lights, who does not change like shifting shadows" (James 1.17).

In the love of Christ,
—Apostle Quail-Child

# A FRIEND'S HEALING TESTIMONY

I pray God speaks to you through this testimony. I can confirm to you that it was written in Spirit.

My girlfriend and I moved to the big city and got jobs after she graduated. We bought a house and started building our lives together. I was still in school for several years after that as I had taken a break for a while. We got engaged and began to grow even closer together. I don't remember exactly when this happened, but she delivered some very devastating news to me. She said she did not believe in God anymore. She said she had known for a while, but she was too afraid to tell me because she thought I would leave her. She said after going to college and learning about the history of the world and new perspectives on science she didn't think it was possible for there to be a God based on the theory of evolution. Despite me not walking with God or actively practicing my faith at the time I was seriously distraught because I knew deep down that there is most definitely a God. I told her I needed to think and process what she told me for a few days. We didn't talk much during this time. I considered ending our relationship, but I loved her too much. In my mind I was basically deciding to either choose God or her. I was convinced that if I chose to stay with her, I would be relinquishing my right to ever get into Heaven. The pressure was so high I can't even describe what I was feeling. I knew I wouldn't leave her and the thought of the impending doom of me going to Hades was the scariest thing I have ever been through in my life. Things were very tense and she was scared to death that I was going to leave her. I finally sat down and had a conversation with her and told her that I wasn't going anywhere. There it was, I did it, I turned my back completely on God. I committed the unforgiveable sin. I made the conscious decision to choose her over God knowing that it would condemn me to Hades. This was the Unforgivable Sin that I was taught about in Sunday school. I was taught that we were all promised at least one chance to accept Christ and that if we said no or consciously decided to turn our back on Him that it was unforgiveable and that you would go to Hades. I can't begin to describe to you what this felt like and what it did to me over the next several months. She never got comfortable; she saw how much I struggled with it and thought I would eventually leave. We got into a huge argument one day and she questioned whether I still loved her because I seemed so much different after she told me she didn't believe anymore. I said to her, "I chose you over God, I condemned myself to Hades so that I could stay with you! Whether you believe in God or not, I do, and if that doesn't prove my love for you than nothing ever will." I could tell right away that it sunk in quickly, and soon after she became comfortable with me again.

I finished school and we got married soon after. The next few years consisted of a downward spiral of greed, pride, sadness, and regret. To be clear, at the time I felt like I was stepping up in life. I was making more money and we were building a life together. There were good and bad times mixed in there, and there were a lot of times where I thought we were happy. Looking back, I can surely tell you, there was no joy. I was so wrapped up in life that I didn't even notice we were spiraling. I started taking anti-depressants and it just seemed like the way life was supposed to go. Little did I know, God was already hard at work breaking me down so He could build me back up.

A few years passed by and the sting of what had happened finally went away. I was in a bad place at work, stressed to the max, working

70+ hours per week, and on the verge of a nervous breakdown. An opportunity presented itself for us to move out of state, make a bunch more money, and start new lives and we took it. This opportunity didn't work out and we ended up moving to yet another state and trying to start all over again shortly after. Over a year of agony and depression passed as we tried to climb out from underneath a mountain of debt. My job was terrible and so was my wife's. We were both working for bad people, and we couldn't go anywhere because we were broke. I was in a dark place, considering suicide and wondering how I ever got to where I was, rock bottom. I was sitting in my living room one day waiting on my wife to get home and I was bawling my eyes out thinking about how bad things were and the kind of life I used to have. I started to think about how I would actually end my life and for some reason I thought to myself, I haven't prayed in a long time, I used to pray so much. I knew God was through with me and that it wasn't going to work but I gave it a shot because I was scared of dying. I begged God to make things better and I told Him I was sorry for what I had done. I started praying more and it wasn't immediate, but sometime after I finally landed a decent job. I was on some pretty heavy anti-depressants at the time and my wife was too. It took several months of working there before I started to feel like a human being again and I was completely broken down and pretty much void of any self-pride.

My new coworker at the new job was retiring soon so they hired a guy to take his place. I met this new guy sometime around March of 2018. We hit it off right from the start and became friends. We liked the same kind of music and we had similar tastes in many different things. I started noticing how joyful he was all the time in spite of many hardships throughout his life. He was very boastful about God and often talked about his faith. He would always say, "Blessed by The Best no stress", and "Hello my brother from another mother but from the same Heavenly Father," and you can't forget "count it all joy." We had multiple conversations about God which were usually initiated by me. At the time I didn't know why I was drawn to him but God's spirit was alive within him and it was calling out to me despite my ignorance. I didn't even know what the Holy Spirit was at this time in my life. I had never learned that the Holy Spirit existed within me. My new friend encouraged me to reignite my walk and start reading my Bible and receiving it in spirit. I started asking him to pray for me and people in my family and he asked the same of me. He started asking me to read specific scriptures and passages based on what was going on in my life. I would always go over and sit in the chair next to his desk when something was weighing on me and just being close to the spirit that was resonating from him gave me answers, comfort, and healing. Each time we had one of these talks God was speaking to me and I didn't even know it, and every time I left that chair I was relieved and my questions were answered. My anxiety got so bad one day I actually broke down in tears in the office at work in front of my friend. He laid his hand on my shoulder and said a prayer. It wasn't long after when I started learning to trust God and I could see that I was going through peaks and valleys in my walk. I didn't really understand it yet, but I was going from "glory to glory". Each time things got bad, I lost faith, and then God picked me back up. Soon it started to sink in that He was refining me and that I needed to start truly trusting in His plans for me. I realized that when I read the Bible and received it in spirit, it was supernatural, and He was speaking directly to me. This was definitely a game changer. If you take anything from this testimony, know that the supernatural experience of God teaching you through His word and confirming to you through the Holy Spirit is a key factor in your walk. My coworker was helping me with prayer and by pointing out scriptures that God put on his heart for me. I still had this deep dark sinking feeling that I was un-redeemable. I pretty much decided that I was willing to try and get back in good standing with God but I didn't hold out much hope that it would actually happen. One thing was weird though, I wasn't sure why God would take the time to teach me about His Holy Spirit and provide so much wisdom and comfort to someone who had committed the unforgiveable sin. Then one day it happened, God spoke to me through a series of thoughts and songs. It was the most electrifying experience I have ever had in my entire life. It felt like someone hooked me up to a battery and charged me to a thousand percent. I was experiencing Joy, for the first time ever in my entire life, TRUE JOY. I heard no audible words from God, I saw no images of Him in front of me, I had no tangible proof and I didn't need any then and I don't need any now. I can tell you with absolute certainty, He spoke to me that day and it changed me. I received it supernaturally and it was the most glorious feeling you could ever imagine. He told me I was going to be successful in my journey to Heaven. He said I was going to be his warrior. He said I was redeemed and that I was not too far gone. He told me it was going to be terrifying and that He would give me the courage to move forward despite my fear. I tell you now, looking back, He told the truth. He got me off those anti-depressants and He filled me with His Spirit. I am still on my journey and there are good times and bad but you can be sure that I know exactly where I am going when I die. I never thought it was possible, I thought I was toast, but He saved me and if He can do that He can save you too.

I feel it is important to let you know that I'm writing this to you now from my original town where this story began in the big city. We're back home, close to our families, and I'm at the same job I was at before and I am very happy with my wife. There are still a lot of bumps in the road but God keeps me on the path and He confirmed to me not too long ago that He was going to save her too. Say a prayer for us both as we move forward and closer to God.

One more thing in closing, I experienced God telling me I had not committed the unforgiveable sin before I even knew what the unforgiveable sin was. I didn't learn about this until a short time ago when my brother from another mother but from the same Heavenly Father told me about this book he was writing, and God put it on his heart to give a sermon on the very subject. I received a very powerful Spiritual confirmation from God during that sermon and He confirmed to me what the Unforgiveable Sin actually is. Like God has a tendency to do, He referenced it back to many other readings and events from my life and gave me 100% confirmation that I had never even come close to committing the unforgiveable sin. If it wasn't too late for me, it's not too late for you! God loves you enough to save your soul regardless of your past. Check your pride, get on your knees, and ask God to save your life. All glory goes to God for this book and this testimony, Amen.

—Wade Franklin

# FOREWORD

There needs to be more verbal or written teaching about the subject of the Unforgiveable Sin, as well as Sin period. As far as I can tell, in the twenty-first century and the Millennium, few have dealt with it extensively with the aspects of the Unforgiveable Sin or sin in general nor deliverance from sin. The book *Unforgiveable Sin* will help the Body of Christ and the people of God to identify what is the Unforgivable Sin and show the Body how men in the Old and New Testaments committed the act of Unforgiveable Sin and the consequence of committing such sin.

God gave the Holy Spirit to the believer to help us in this walk of life; in the book *Unforgivable Sin*, Pastor Quail-Child shows the Body how we can go against the leading of the Holy Spirit, and this can cause the believer to commit the sin of blaspheme against The Holy Spirit. The word of the Lord says, "Verily I say unto you, All sins shall be forgiven unto the sons of men, and blasphemies wherewith soever they shall blaspheme. But he that shall blaspheme against the Holy Ghost hath never forgiveness but is in danger of eternal damnation. Because they said, He hath an unclean spirit" (Mark 3:28 - 30). For years we were taught that if we mock or make fun of the saints dancing, speaking in tongues, praising God, and laying on hands, we were blaspheming against the Holy Ghost. No, to blaspheme, as Pastor Quail-Child shows us in this book, is when we go against his instructions and lie to him that we know that the sin of blaspheming the Holy Ghost will never be forgiven in this life or the life to come. Pastor Quail-Child showed the body of Christ how the sin of unforgiveable is carried out by some. He also points out how some who committed the sin of unforgivable were removed from whatever office they were in, and God removed the anointing for them as well.

I pray that you read this book with an open mind, heart, and spirit, and we may hear what the Spirit of the Lord is saying to the church.

—Apostle Spear of Battle
Founder – Trumpet of Praise Fellowship International

# AUTHOR'S INSPIRATION
# FOR THE BOOK

This book is inspired by my personal experience dealing with the teaching, counseling and preaching on the Unforgiveable Sin over the years, solely guided and influenced by The Holy Spirit. The Lord has burdened my heart with the understanding of how the spirits of deception and ignorance have profoundly infiltrated the church in these end-of-end times – with doctrine being created that deviates from the infallible Holy Bible truth, which has caused false teaching and unfortunately false learning as the recipients of this teaching ... and quite frankly, avoidance on this topic due to ignorance and lack of knowledge. As such, but not on my own authority or knowledge, The Holy Spirit has charged me to write on this topic. Bringing greater understanding and spiritual knowledge to this spiritually critical topic among the Body of Christ, but also among the unbelievers in the World who have been discouraged or otherwise deceived on this topic as well - hindering their opportunity at salvation. Thus, as Apostle Paul warns: "I urge you, brothers and sisters, to watch out for those who cause divisions and put obstacles in your way that are contrary to the teaching you have learned. Keep away from them. For such people are not serving our Lord Christ, but their own appetites. By smooth talk and flattery, they deceive the minds of naive people" (Romans 16:17-18).

In contrast, not only spiritually naïve people have been deceived, but also ministry leaders who have leaned on their own understanding and have introduced a deviant doctrine. Case in point: an elder and associate pastor in a small church who also leads a Bible study on Sundays, even to this day, once told me: "There is no unforgivable sin ... the only sin that is not forgiven is unrepented sin". I will keep his name out of this. Do note, however, this elder has been teaching Bible school for many years. Important thing to know here, deception does not discriminate! Let that sink in deeply! Another example ... a dear friend who is also in the ministry since childhood, over thirty years now, who's name will remain anonymous, once told me: "Blaspheme of The Holy Spirit is not in the gospels or scriptures ... it is a man-made doctrine". Seriously, and he was quite adamite about it and would not accept loving correction either. We know that Jesus' himself spoke and taught his disciples on this sin in three out of the four Gospels (Matthew 12.31-32, Luke 12.10 and Mark 3.28-29).

The point I'm trying to make here is not to insult or degrade my brothers' walk in the Body of Christ or imply how they serve in the ministry is unfaithful – not at all! But raise spiritual attention to how real this issue is. I trust that in spirit as you are reading now, you are starting to feel the burden and provocation The Holy Spirit has placed on my heart as an obedient and yielded vessel to take up this spiritual privilege to honor and uphold His intended teaching on this topic and help you attain its uncompromised truth with supernatural understanding.

I will go deeper into the "why" this issue exists among ministry leaders in later chapters of the book, but the following will give you a preliminary understanding. The Word of God is not intended to be read literally on your own understanding, but spiritually yielded as you read so that it comes alive and brings forth conviction that refines us: the good news that uplifts us and the hope and trust that builds our faith - supernaturally penetrating our very soul and conscience. As mentioned in The Book of Hebrews: "For the word of God is alive and active. Sharper than any double-edged sword, it penetrates even to dividing soul and spirit, joints and marrow; it judges the thoughts and attitudes of the heart" (Hebrews 4.12). Therefore, when the Word of God is read in any other way than in spirit, its spiritual content and intended knowledge for us is greatly compromised. Jesus said it like this: "But the Advocate, the Holy Spirit, whom the Father will send in my name, will teach you all things and will remind you of everything I have said to you" (John 14.26).

My inspiration doesn't stop there … there was a false conviction that had fallen upon several brothers while I was preaching on this topic in a men's recovery home in Phoenix, AZ. The Lord began to speak to me, and He quickened my heart and spirit to combat the evil manifestation of this false conviction that had infiltrated the sanctuary. However, He wanted me to know that by reading strictly from His Word, this sin can be easily misunderstood. Prior to this, the Lord had been speaking to me how the devil has been wreaking havoc among His children throughout the World – planting unfruitful seeds of deception which have propagated into ignorance over the many centuries following the resurrection of Christ Jesus and severely diluting the truth. Unfortunately, these seeds have produced and continue to produce unholy fruit – as it's The Father's will that all would listen to His son's teaching – but the devil interferes with this doctrine. He, the devil, deceives and brings forth the spirits of deception, ignorance, avoidance and now we have learned – false conviction. False conviction comes from oneself, and not by divine power under the unction of The Holy Spirit. For example, one of the brother's while I was preaching on this topic asked: "Why should I serve God if I have committed this Unforgiveable Sin?" The fact of the matter is, he didn't – he didn't even come anywhere close to it. Mind you, this brother claimed to have been a pagan who worshiped Azteca religion since childhood. He was a product of his environment and upbringing, unaware of the truth; therefore, ignorance does not come close to committing this sin, as it is written in scriptures: "I thank Christ Jesus our Lord, who has given me strength, that he considered me trustworthy, appointing me to his service. Even though I was once a blasphemer and a persecutor and a violent man, I was shown mercy because I acted in ignorance and unbelief. The grace of our Lord was poured out on me abundantly, along with the faith and love that are in Christ Jesus" (1 Timothy 1:12-14). At the time my brother was a new member in the recovery program, into his mid-thirties, but was radically changed into a new man of God following some months later. It is with condolences I share now that this brother has since gone to be with the Lord in the summer of 2019. He had been battling some severe medical conditions.

I sincerely hope and trust that you are now starting to truly understand the depth of my inspiration and conviction, brought on me by The Holy Spirit, to teach on this topic. Let's trust in Him together, believing that His delivering power is upon us and will faithfully break the chains of deception on this topic, bringing forth supernatural understanding, encouragement and doctrinal reconciliation to the World. Yes, the World too, as it is written: "For God so loved the world that he gave his one and only Son, that whoever believes in him shall not perish but have eternal life" (John 3.16). Additionally, I trust this teaching will help those in the World suffering from unbelief and will also be encouraged by this spiritually synoptic teaching on the Unforgivable Sin, and that the release of new hope, trust and the knowledge of life eternal will be more greatly appreciated, reverenced, honored and ultimately attained through the Glory of King Jesus, The Holy Spirit, and God the Father in Heaven, amen!

# EXHORTATION

For the believers in Christ Jesus or not, my heart hurts and is very burdened with His pain knowing many in the World have been deceived and discouraged by false doctrine, teaching and avoidance due to ignorance regarding the 'Unforgiveable Sin'. Jesus indicates this unforgiveable sin as "blaspheme against the Holy Spirit" in three of the four Gospels of the New Testament, which are Matthew 12.31-32, Luke 12.10 and Mark 3.28-29. The sad but interesting thing among "believers" is that many of us have never felt and fellowshipped with The Holy Spirt. So, before we can even come close to having a spiritually comprehensive and accurate understanding of this sin, I must attempt to lead and usher you into the presence of The Holy Spirit. In the Book of Revelation Jesus continuously mentions, "Whoever has ears, let them hear what the Spirit says to the churches" (Example: Revelation 2.7). There is a critically spiritual reason why Jesus emphasizes this multiple times, because He is desiring us who choose to read the Revelation of His testimony in Spirit to have the reading come alive and obtain all that He wants to bless us with in terms of His truth made supernaturally known … if we don't receive it in Spirit we will not receive His fullness of the truth. Likewise with this book, since it is written under the unction of Holy Spirit through my yielded vessel for His glory, you will not receive the fullness He has intended for you with respect to this topic, Unforgiveable Sin, unless you open your heart to receive what the Holy Spirit intends for you to learn and fully understand regarding it. Therefore, I pray (join me and receive):

Heavenly Father – Creator of the Heavens and Earth,

I pray in Your son Jesus' name – my Lord and Savior, that You would supernaturally touch the hearts of Your children, whether believers of Him or not, with the expressed love of His finished works at the cross of Calvary, which was and still is and forevermore unconditional. I say this knowing my limited ability to pray as a mere mortal, but Father use me as a vessel for Your honor and glory to usher in the presence of Your Holy Spirit as my brothers and sisters read this prayer right now – my faith is confident in Your power to touch and transform even among the perceived most difficult of unbelievers, but even the believers who lean more on their own understanding than Your Holy Spirt. Father – bless Your children according to Your perfect will, with an undeniable fellowship that can only be obtained through Your divine touch in this very moment and the moments to come as they read the rest of this book. Amen and amen.

To first address the Blood-Washed Believers claiming to be a part of the Body of Christ, but also to encourage them and the unbelievers together, I sincerely ask that you dare to ask yourself this: Do I understand what the Unforgiveable Sin really is? Be honest with yourself and to Him in His presence – He, The Spirit of Truth, who can and will bless you if you're honest and willing in heart. This question is not aimed to belittle you, as the spirit of deception will try and trick you into believing, but to spiritually probe your own heart with The Holy Spirit's help to determine your true knowledge of this topic or lack thereof. The first component of this synoptic teaching and deepening of your understanding of the Unforgivable Sin must be a tapping into fellowship with The Holy Spirit as you read and hear what the Spirit desires for you to learn. That said, this exhortation will continue to lay out with respect to The Holy Spirit to align your "Spirit Man" within you, with the Father's. Yes, we prayed for this earlier, but now it's time to corroborate the Holy Bible along with the first Holy Scriptures, *The Books of Enoch*, which preceded the Holy Bible in its Parts I and II, and The Holy Spirit as He reveals the truth on this topic – bringing all three of these spiritual components into harmonious alignment supernaturally. Some may be thinking now, why the Books of Enoch – they're not part of the Bible … but on the contrary, they are. For example, reference Jude 1:14–15. Who is Jude? It is widely believed that he is the brother of Jesus Christ Himself. So, if the Book of Enoch where this scripture is quoted from was good in the New Testament of the Bible (1 Enoch Ch 1:9), why not for this book? To help with a scriptural sense as mentioned in The Book of John: "The Word became flesh and made his dwelling among us. We have seen his glory, the glory of the one and only Son, who came from the Father, full of grace and truth" (John 1.14). Trust me, while under the unction of Holy Spirit, starting with this exhortation on Him, The Holy Spirit, is key and foundational to understanding the rest of this book and the full truth Biblically of the Unforgiveable Sin. The Word of God is not intended to be taken literally with man's limited interpretation and understanding, but rather made perfect in spirit and truth supernaturally. That is why the scripture says: "For the word of God is alive and active. Sharper than any double-edged sword, it penetrates even to dividing soul and spirit, joints and marrow; it judges the thoughts and attitudes of the heart" (Hebrews 4.12).

# INTRODUCTION

Now let's shift gears in Spirit to glean from the Father's heart in the Old Testament (OT) as to what this Unforgivable Sin looks like with spiritual vividness. It must be made known, that in order to fully understand what this sin is we must dive into the waters of OT, namely with Moses' testimony where it is initially committed by him and referred to later by the Father in Heaven. In this Biblically synoptic view in OT, this Unforgivable Sin will be defined in detail as represented by the heart of the Father, God Almighty Himself, while looking into the actions of Moses in detail where this sin was first committed.

Following the definition, it will be revealed what the blended components that makeup this Unforgiveable Sin are – very important to know alongside the Biblical definition. These are the following components, and they will be carefully and spiritually examined:

- This sin is committed by a man or woman of God who fellowships with The Holy Spirit;
  - He or she is active in one or more of the gifts of The Holy Spirit;
  - He or she must break faith and reject God's holiness in the presence of others before God; and
  - It's rooted in and caused by manifested self-pride by the God-fearing person(s).

The spiritual knowledge made known by the components of the Unforgivable Sin will lay the foundation for understanding the extent of who and how this sin is committed against The Holy Spirit, and provide the spiritual means for another evaluation in OT where this sin was committed by King Saul (King David's predecessor) – testing your knowledge from the reader's vantage for increased spiritual edification. I say this not by my authority, but the Lord's, as it is written: "Dear friends, do not believe every spirit, but test the spirits to see whether they are from God, because many false prophets have gone out into the world" (1 John 4.1). Make no mistake – many false teachers of the scriptures are out in the World as well. We must be certain the teaching is divine, but that it's understanding revealed to you as the reader is divine as well – both are spiritually crucial.

Another OT account of the Unforgiveable Sin is the testimony of King Saul. We will venture into this story to heighten our understanding. This view will bridge all the similarities between Moses and Saul to deepen our knowledge and understanding according to the Heavenly Father's will. Make no mistake, by now we will earn the understanding of the definition of the Unforgivable Sin – made plainly and simply as The Holy Spirit reinforces.

Now that we know the heart of the Father concerning the Unforgivable Sin, I ask you: are you interested in knowing what happened to Moses when he was commanded to die by God Almighty on Mount Nebo for his sin? In this teaching you will glean first from God's command as referred to in The Book of Deuteronomy regarding His prophetic message to His servant Moses. Next, which is of great spiritual importance, we will glean from God and His verdict of Moses as revealed in The Book of 3 Enoch (The Hebrew Book). This will also give some spiritual understanding of the reinforced system the Father has regarding His heavenly hosts and the divine justice system setup that He exercises (like today's court system) – this is really an added spiritual benefit that highlights His merciful and gracious character. Understanding at this point will be revealed with great light and clarity on the fight between one of the arch angels of heaven, Michael, and Satan regarding Moses' body after he died at

God's command – this will be coined and revealed from The Book of Jude. This is important to understanding the spiritual controversy in the Heavenlies by the ultimate verdict God made on the account of Moses. This will enlighten us and provide spiritual appreciation for God's confirmation of judgement pertaining to His mercies and grace that truly endures forever (Ref. Psalm 136.1). However, this will also be backed up with exhortation not to flirt or otherwise take for granted His mercies and grace once we come into Blood Covenant with Him, as it is written: "Do not put the Lord your God to the test as you did at Massah" (Deuteronomy 6.16).

Now that we have a spiritually solid foundation laid as to the Father's heart regarding what the Unforgiveable Sin looks like as we gleaned from OT, we now segue into NT and pinpoint the committals on several accounts of the Unforgivable Sin. All Gospels take into written account this sin having been committed first by Judas Iscariot. Make no mistake, all 12 of Jesus' disciples dishonored Him just before His crucifixion; however, Judas betrays Him first by giving into the spirit of lukewarm, followed by the kiss of betrayal – all of which demonstrating the breaking of faith and forfeiting God's holiness. All this will be spiritually broken down in granular detail, as to coin the spiritual severity of this disgraceful act. Secondly, we will venture into the Book of Acts and analyze this sin in a couple other accounts, starting with the married couple, Ananias and Sapphira, who withheld money from the church and lied about it in the active presence of The Holy Spirit. Then we will finish this evaluation with the account of King Herod who withheld God's glory as the crowd he was addressing mentioned to the effect: "he speaks like a god," and did not immediately admonish them. Again, we'll investigate these NT accounts of the committal of the Unforgiveable Sin and analyze their similarities, and how lukewarm is the seed that swiftly progresses into the breaking of faith and forfeiting God's holiness when given into this sin.

Next, is an evaluation of the quickening of Jesus' mercy and grace as He preserves the spiritual health of the church regarding this sin. It is important to understand here, we as His co-heirs in the Blood

Covenant with Him, are the church now ... as it is written: "Don't you know that you yourselves are God's temple and that God's Spirit dwells in your midst? If anyone destroys God's temple, God will destroy that person; for God's temple is sacred, and you together are that temple" (1 Corinthians 3.16-17). "And he is the head of the body, the church ..." (Colossians 1.18).

Next, I'll expose the deception of the devil under the anointment of The Holy Spirit and how this deception is aimed to lead as many in the world into Hades regarding this Unforgiveable Sin. If he, the devil, can convince your conscience that you committed it (when you really didn't), he can then influence your life under his invisible deceptive spirits to sin and value the worldly ways which lead to death, than God's Kingdom values, which lead to life eternal. Therefore, as it is written: "For the message of the cross is foolishness to those who are perishing, but to us who are being saved it is the power of God" (1 Corinthians 1:18). We know the devil is a liar, he's the prince of the world, but true love exposes this truth and casts out all fear (Ref. 1 John 4:18). So, the encouraging thing is knowing the truth, so we are no longer in chains of bondage to our own sinful desires and unknowingly governed by the devil, but closer to the release and deliverance from living to sin as the Lord desires for us ... in other words, live according to God's will and not the devil's, as the scripture says: "For our struggle is not against flesh and blood, but against the rulers, against the authorities, against the powers of this dark world and against the spiritual forces of evil in the heavenly realms" (Ephesians 6:12). The truth sets us free!

Time to break the devil's curse of deception regarding his false conviction of the Unforgivable Sin. As mentioned above, the truth sets us free. Let the Bible coin a very encouraging note: "So if the Son sets you free, you will be free indeed" (John 8:36). The truth breaks all the devil's curses. Although from the time Jesus walked the earth till now, blaspheme against The Holy Spirit and the truth regarding it departed much from His children and He desires to recalibrate us spiritually. Know the truth! Break the curse! This closing focus will bring clarity to how the generation of Jesus' time through the many generations up to now has been progressively deceived and now more than ever before. Let us be blessed by His Holy Spirit as many more of God's children will be set free!

# UNFORGIVABLE SIN DEFINED

Let's journey now into the testimony of Moses and define this sin that Jesus referred to as blaspheme against The Holy Spirit, which is unforgivable. To extract the definition from the Bible we must first pinpoint the committal, which was initially committed by Moses. Therefore, let's investigate The Book of Numbers, chapter 20 and versus 9–13:

"So Moses took the staff from the LORD's presence, just as he commanded him. He and Aaron gathered the assembly together in front of the rock and Moses said to them, 'Listen, you rebels, must we bring you water out of this rock'? Then Moses raised his arm and struck the rock twice with his staff. Water gushed out, and the community and their livestock drank. But the LORD said to Moses and Aaron, "Because you did not trust in me enough to honor me as holy in the sight of the Israelites, you will not bring this community into the land I give them." These were the waters of Meribah, where the Israelites quarreled with the LORD and where he was proved holy among them."

When Moses said: "must we bring you water out of this rock?" This was the committal by Moses, as he made it look as if the miracle, sign, and wonder was by his and Aaron's doings alone. The fact is, God was with him as He was at the burning bush where He called Moses into the ministry; as He was at the Red Sea where He split the waters for the Israelites to cross safely from the opposition of the Egyptians who they were being freed from; as He was at the Rock of

Meribah the first time where Moses struck the Rock in obedience to receive drinking water – in all these miracles and many others, signs and wonders it was God by His Holy Spirit working in and through Moses as a yielded, humble vessel and servant of God – who Moses carefully gave God all the glory as He divinely deserved. Thus, this shines light to the act of having committed the Unforgiveable Sin against God Almighty, blessed be Him. This is the first example in the Bible where this sin is committed – in other words, Moses was the first servant of God who had committed it.

Symbolically and yet spiritually, it is important to know that the Son of Man, Jesus Christ, was the Rock (and yet still is The Rock) – representing salvation which poured the water of life for the Israelites to drink from. This is important knowing that here in the Old Testament, before the Son of Man came to earth in physical form through the Virgin Mary, the Holy Trinity is in full representation in this example – given only by Spirit, not human interpretation. Let me explain ... I share that here for those who are not as familiar with the Bible spiritually and its many parallels between Old and New Testaments, and the many prophetic references that point to Jesus before He ever came to the earth in human form. Amazing! This also, however, demonstrates the intense arrogance on the part of Moses (caused by the spirit of self-pride), knowing well what he did to self-exalt himself for the awe of self-glory before the Israelites and in the active presence of The Holy Spirit, God Almighty and His Beloved Son. Just in case you are wondering ... how did Moses know Jesus before He came? As it was spoken by Jesus Himself as He was having a rebuttal with the Jewish leaders who at the time were accusing Him of breaking the Sabbath Day where He defends Himself by saying: "But do not think I will accuse you before the Father. Your accuser is Moses, on whom your hopes are set. If you believed Moses, you would believe me, for he wrote about me. But since you do not believe what he wrote, how are you going to believe what I say" (John 5:45-47)?

It is equally important that we realize here that there were two instances where the Israelites received water at the Rock of

Meribah – at two different times. The first time Moses did exactly as God so instructed, and when the miracle, sign and wonder occurred, he was careful to give all glory to God in the sight of his fellow Israelites, men, women and children – this is found in the Book of Exodus, chapter 17. To be clear, it was on the second occasion at the Rock of Meribah where he sinned against God Almighty, blessed be He, as noted earlier (ref. Numbers 20:9-13).

To coin a New Testament point of disgrace of the same manner which Moses committed by this sin, Biblically, to further stress the nature of his sin: "It is impossible for those who have once been enlightened, who have tasted the heavenly gift, who have shared in the Holy Spirit, who have tasted the goodness of the word of God and the powers of the coming age and who have fallen away, to be brought back to repentance. To their loss they are crucifying the Son of God all over again and subjecting him to public disgrace" (Hebrews 6:4-6).

Now it is time to define what this Unforgivable Sin is made plainly and simply as The Holy Spirit and the Word of God graciously give it. That said there is a combination of elements, that combined, define the sin based on the acts of Moses – but is revealing from the heart of The Father in Heaven as follows: Then the LORD said to Moses, "Go up this mountain in the Abarim Range and see the land I have given the Israelites. After you have seen it, you too will be gathered to your people, as your brother Aaron was, for when the community rebelled at the waters in the Desert of Zin, both of you disobeyed my command to honor me as holy before their eyes" (Numbers 27:12-14). The way Holy Spirit gives it in this piece of scripture first is: **Forfeiting God's Holiness in the sight of the Israelites and in the presence of Holy Spirit**. This, however, only encapsulates half of the sin's definition. Let me explain …

Combined with:

"On that same day the LORD told Moses, 'Go up into the Abarim Range to Mount Nebo in Moab, across from Jericho, and view Canaan, the land I am giving the Israelites as their own possession. There on the mountain that you have climbed you will die and be gathered to your people, just as your brother Aaron died on Mount Hor and was gathered to his people. This is because both of you broke faith with me in the presence of the Israelites at the waters of Meribah Kadesh in the Desert of Zin and because you did not uphold my holiness among the Israelites. Therefore, you will see the land only from a distance; you will not enter the land I am giving to the people of Israel'" (Deuteronomy 32:48-52). The way He gives it here in Spirit is: **Breaking faith with God in the sight of the Israelites and in the active presence of The Holy Spirit**. However, in this example the Lord defines it fully, but we used both references to encapsulate all of God's definition to bridge it all together chronologically from the Bible.

Therefore, the Biblical definition in its entirety of this sin Jesus refers to in the New Testament as: *Unforgiveable Sin*, is as follows: **Breaking faith and forfeiting God's holiness in the presence of people and in the active presence of The Holy Spirit**. Again, it was the Spirt of God who worked in and through Moses and his brother Aaron to perform the many miracles, signs and wonders – so in committing this spiritually disgraceful act it is key to know it is in the "active" presence of The Holy Spirit. Thus, to bridge the Biblical reference earlier on this topic with respect to Jesus the Son of God – it was the power of God, The Holy Spirit, that raised Jesus from the dead that Moses committed the Unforgivable Sin in His presence ... active presence – meaning, where God through His Holy Spirit performed the miracle, sign and wonder where the Water of Life flowed through the Rock of Salvation a second time in the dry desert where Moses was leading the stiff-necked and rebellious Israelites out of and towards a new land God referred to as: "flowing with milk and honey" (ref. Exodus 3:17).

It is trusted that at this point you are well acclimated with the definition of the Unforgivable Sin, also known as Blaspheme Against The Holy Spirit, which was defined by God in the Old Testament references noted hereof. Next, it will be discussed in detail the components of this sin to bring great spiritual enlightenment and understanding which accompanies its definition.

# HEART OF THE FATHER

Father God, blessed be He, desires His children to have an understanding of His character. It is written early on in scripture: "So God created mankind in his own image, in the image of God he created them; male and female he created them" (Genesis 1:27). We, mere mortals are created in God's image, an image is a reflection ... so when God says we are made in His image - we are a reflection of Him. Amazing! Therefore, His character which we are intended to reflect, both physically and spiritually, helps us to understand that we share a relationship with Him by nature – how much more when we get to know Him with a spiritual concentration? No better way to get to know our Heavenly Father than by reading in spirit His written responses especially in the Old Testament. In this synoptic view of understanding The Father's heart, I will take you deep into Old Testament waters - it will draw us close to Him bringing forth great revelation with a deep understanding of His heart.

Following will reveal the makeup of the Unforgivable Sin by delineating its three specific components, along with the root cause, explain the revelation of this Unforgivable Sin's curse – revealed only through The Father's Spirit, and close with another Old Testament example which will test the retained knowledge of this teaching. These are spiritually crucial to understand – and to understand from God's own heart – this is revealed in Old Testament and in Spirit. Yes, we've learned in detail what the definition of this Unforgivable Sin is, but that alone does not provide a relational and spiritual connection with the Father's heart, along with the truth about this Unforgivable Sin. As mentioned in my inspiration for writing this book, much of the truth has been diluted over the years since Jesus rose from the grave – that has been a mystery for the Body of Christ's majority, but that will change for His glory. Therefore, understanding The Father's heart on this Unforgivable Sin will bring great spiritual revelation, as we compassionately feel from the heart of God Himself – as His children – as His prized and created reflection spiritually.

# COMPONENTS

Who commits this grievous act of blaspheme against The Holy Spirit? If you thought it could be committed by anybody, I lovingly tell you – you are wrong! This unforgivable act is only committed by a man or woman who once was or is God-fearing. In other words, this act is committed by a servant of the Lord - a man or women of God. In the previous topic discussed in this Book, blaspheme against The Holy Spirit was Biblically defined as: *Breaking faith and forfeiting God's holiness in the presence of people and in the active presence of The Holy Spirit.* Thus, following will provide a spiritual synopsis of the three elements that comprise and make up the character of the one who commits this sin, which are as follows:

1. As mentioned, it's <u>committed by a God-fearing person</u>;
2. This God-fearing person <u>fellowships with Holy Spirit</u>; and
3. This God-fearing person is <u>activated with one or more gifts of The Holy Spirit</u>.

To synoptically detail these elements of the Unforgivable Sin, Moses' testimony will be used as it was earlier in the book to define it because he was the first to commit it, and I believe the Heart of the Father in Heaven, blessed be He, is best revealed with clarity in Moses' testimony.

Just before we get into the elements, let us pray against the spirit of skepticism, as The Holy Spirit revealed to me that many at this point will be skeptically questioning: How can a Godly person sin unforgivably?

Heavenly Father – Creator of the Heavens and Earth,

I pray in Your son Jesus' name – my Lord and Savior, that Your simplicity of the truth would befall all flesh, my dear brother's and sister's, who read and take part in this prayer. By Your Spirit, we declare the dismantling of all spirits of skepticism, that Your truth on this matter will be supernaturally revealed and understood to those who receive it. Amen.

Like Moses, this sin is committed by a God-fearing person, man or woman. Obviously, Moses was a man in this example who first committed it - at least with respect to the common Bible, comprised of the 66 books between Old and New Testaments. Certainly, Moses was not the first God-fearing person referred to in the Bible, but he commits the Unforgivable Sin first – he, meaning, a man born from a woman's womb – a mortal human being like you and me. I stress this so as not to get it confused with angelic spirits who had fallen from God's glory in the Heavenly realm, namely, Satan – who once was a ministering spirit in the Heavenlies, who later God rejected from among His angelical holy-hosts and cast him down to the abyss (which later became part of Mother Earth as we know it today - The Sea). Certainly, Satan is the first to commit an eternally abominable and Unforgivable Sin even before man had ever been created (Adam), but we are keeping this teaching within the confines of a flesh-and-blood person, in this case, Moses and several who succeeded him later – which best relates to you and me as mortal humans.

How do we know Moses was a God-fearing man? Well, Moses was chosen by God to carry out the mission of leading the Israelites out of Egyptian slavery, and into God's Promised Land – flowing with milk and honey. Surly God is not going to use a leader who doesn't know Him to carry out many signs, miracles and wonders that glorify Him – even the Word of God says that God, Himself, spoke to Moses: "The LORD would speak to Moses face to face, as one speaks to a friend" (Exodus 33:11). Up until the time where

Moses committed the Unforgivable Sin, he was always careful to reverence God – reverencing God is out of love such as: appreciation, obedience, but also with trembling with fear. Moses feared God by these attributes of love, but make no mistake, also with trembling … for example, take the burning bush where God first spoke to Moses, as it is written: "When the LORD saw that he had gone over to look, God called to him from within the bush, "Moses! Moses"! And Moses said, "Here I am". "Do not come any closer", God said. "Take off your sandals, for the place where you are standing is holy ground". Then he said, "I am the God of your father, the God of Abraham, the God of Isaac and the God of Jacob". At this, Moses hid his face, because he was afraid to look at God (Exodus 3:4-6). Fast forward now to where God spoke to Moses and the entire Israelites at Mount Sinai, where trembling with fear seized them all, including Moses: 'When the people saw the thunder and lightning and heard the trumpet and saw the mountain in smoke, they trembled with fear. They stayed at a distance and said to Moses, 'Speak to us yourself and we will listen. But do not have God speak to us or we will die'. Moses said to the people, 'Do not be afraid. God has come to test you, so that the fear of God will be with you to keep you from sinning'" (Exodus 20:18–20). This event would be spiritually amplified in the New Testament as well: The sight was so terrifying that Moses said, "I am trembling with fear" (Hebrews 12:21).

Moses was a God-fearing man … make no mistake! When he was irrevocably commanded to die, and in fact after he did, it was attributed to him as having been a "servant of the Lord" (Deuteronomy 34:5). In the same chapter of Deuteronomy as the last reference of Moses, to coin his God-fearing character: "Since then, no prophet has risen in Israel like Moses, whom the LORD knew face to face, who did all those signs and wonders the LORD sent him to do in Egypt—to Pharaoh and to all his officials and to his whole land. For no one has ever shown the mighty power or performed the awesome deeds that Moses did in the sight of all Israel" (Deuteronomy 34:10–12).

In bringing this element to closure, I ask: Can fear after death be explained? Let me explain, yes ... as we dive into the 3$^{rd}$ Book of Enoch where Moses after death, and when his spirit ascended into Heaven to be judged, he mentions to Enoch, son of Jared (now referred to as 'Metatron' in the Heavenlies): "I fear lest I bring guiltiness upon myself" (Ch. 15-B V. 5). This is fascinating, and although the Books of Enoch are not in the common Bible, this Holy Scripture – this God-Breathed scripture isolates a moment in time within the Divine Throne Room of God Almighty, where it details Moses' emotions, where yet again, fear of the Lord seized his spirit during judgement. You might already be wondering ... what was God's verdict for Moses – did he go to Heaven or Hades? I am eager to share with you that the answer to that question comes later in the book ... In all spiritual seriousness, don't jump ahead! Rather, let The Great Spirit, The Holy Spirit – The Spirit of God arouse our conscience, heart and Spirit-man within.

Secondly, this sin as mentioned earlier is committed by a God-fearing person who fellowships with The Holy Spirit. To be clear, it is important to understand who The Holy Spirit is. He is a part of the One-God trinity – **As One** – God The Father, God The Son, and God The Holy Spirit. To keep this simple, and to limit any potential for spiritual confusion, which I rebuke in Jesus' name, The Holy Spirit represents our invisible advocate – who is now granted unto us who believe in The Son Jesus, who then pours out the favor of Heaven by and through The Father's will. Jesus has died over 2000 years ago but resurrected to Life and ascended back into the Heavenlies, we now fellowship with Jesus through The Holy Spirit. Hmmm ... well then you might ask, how did it work with respect to The Holy Spirit and Moses' fellowship together since the Bible stated earlier that they, God and Moses, spoke together "face to face"? During this time in Old Testament and all throughout it, God The Father fellowshipped with Moses also through The Holy Spirit ... in either case, The Holy Spirit is invisible and is the same then as He is now ... however, His manifestation can cause physical signs, miracles and wonders. For example, it was the invisible power of The Holy Spirit that split the Dead Sea and created a safe highway for Moses and his people of Israel to escape their Egyptian enemies. The fellowship, like person-to-person or people-to-people, it is through verbal communication, but in addition to that - silent communication. To be clear, person-to-person is primarily verbal communication (sign language, written, etc.) ... person to The Holy Spirit is either verbal or silent communication (but all forms of communication does The Holy Spirit know). I lay this foundation here on fellowshipping with The Holy Spirit to establish a basic point of reference, this is not intended to be suppository teaching and expounding of the subject, but enough to help you get the point. So that from here, you understand the fellowshipping with The Holy Spirit as we venture, yet again, in Moses' testimony with respect to his fellowship with The Holy Spirit.

One of the most spiritually prominent ways Moses fellowshipped with The Holy Spirit was through prayer. There were several times throughout Moses' testimony where he would consult God (through prayer – praying in Spirit to God). This was done by Moses praying to God with outcomes not yet passed. How, might you ask? By faith ... bringing the imaginary into your thoughts – hoping for God's favor on the desired outcome. Moses demonstrates this type of prayer, as one example of many, the first time at the Rock of Meribah where God first provided water out of this Rock for the complaining Israelites, as it is written: "But the people were thirsty for water there, and they grumbled against Moses. They said, 'Why did you bring us up out of Egypt to make us and our children and livestock die of thirst'? Then Moses cried out to the LORD, "What am I to do with these people? They are almost ready to stone me." The LORD answered Moses, "Go out in front of the people. Take with you some of the elders of Israel and take in your hand the staff with which you struck the Nile, and go. I will stand there before you by the rock at Horeb. Strike the rock, and water will come out of it for the people to drink." So Moses did this in the sight of the elders of Israel" (Exodus 17:3–6). Let me help spiritually dissect this awesome moment ... so Moses prayed in spirit and by faith ... he sought God through prayer, through a plea, a form of communication with an invisible God, The Holy Spirit. Yes, God spoke to Moses on what to do, and Moses obeyed … but even this discourse was taken invisibly. God was not seen physically … it was His voice through The Holy Spirit speaking to Moses' conscience supernaturally. Very important we understand this.

To bring this 2nd element to closure, we see clearly how Moses fellowshipped with God through The Holy Spirit. This was demonstrated through prayer, pleading to, and believing with hope in, The Invisible God, blessed be He. The intended outcome thus came to pass, which was the water that was not previously there, became for them to drink. Moses prayed to bring Heaven down, through his fellowship with God (prayer), and received God The Father's favor through his obedience.

As we come to the last element, the third to be exact, which is a God-fearing person who is activated with one or more gifts of The Holy Spirit. What is such a gift or gifts, which is/are given by Holy Spirit? What were Moses' Spirit-giftings? These gifts are distributed to those God wills, as it is written: "There are different kinds of gifts, but the same Spirit distributes them. There are different kinds of service, but the same Lord. There are different kinds of working, but in all of them and in everyone it is the same God at work. Now to each one the manifestation of the Spirit is given for the common good. To one there is given through the Spirit a message of wisdom, to another a message of knowledge by means of the same Spirit, to another faith by the same Spirit, to another gifts of healing by that one Spirit, to another miraculous powers, to another prophecy, to another distinguishing between spirits, to another speaking in different kinds of tongues, and to still another the interpretation of tongues. All these are the work of one and the same Spirit, and he distributes them to each one, just as he determines" (1 Corinthians 12:4–11).

Moses had several Spirt-giftings as a God-fearing servant. One of the nine that was mentioned above in 1 Corinthians, which was Biblically prominent, was the gift of prophecy. In fact, it was depicted in an earlier example when explaining God-fearing from the Book of Deuteronomy chapter 34 verse 10 as follows: "Since then, no prophet has risen in Israel like Moses ..." As Jesus would say, I also say under the unction of The Holy Spirit, "very truly I tell you" – now I say solely - Moses possessed even the following gifts of The Holy Spirit: Scribe (holy author), Prophet, Priestly (holy shepherd), Faith, and Miracles. Let's be careful here though, these gifts are done by The Holy Spirit (invisibly) through Moses (physically) as a vessel, in this example - but applies to all God's elected children who He distributes such gifts. Moses without a shadow of a doubt, was activated with gifts of The Holy Spirit – the third element comprising this Unforgivable Sin.

# ROOT CAUSE

The root cause of the Unforgivable Sin is self-pride of a God-fearing person. We see that when Moses committed this sin, he arrogantly pointed to himself and his brother Aaron for having performed the sign, miracle and wonder that God performed, not Moses and Arron. God's Holy Spirit performed the miracle through Moses' human vessel – a conduit essentially for the Spirit of God to flow through. Similarly, how electricity flows through wire. The power is not the wire itself, but the invisible electricity flowing through it – with power. Let's recap the circumstances, commands and the moment where Moses blasphemed The Holy Spirit, and where Aaron failed to admonish him whereby taking part as an accomplice in this Unforgivable Sin:

"Now there was no water for the community, and the people gathered in opposition to Moses and Aaron. They quarreled with Moses and said, 'If only we had died when our brothers fell dead before the LORD! Why did you bring the LORD's community into this wilderness, that we and our livestock should die here? Why did you bring us up out of Egypt to this terrible place? It has no grain or figs, grapevines or pomegranates. And there is no water to drink'! Moses and Aaron went from the assembly to the entrance to the tent of meeting and fell facedown, and the glory of the LORD appeared to them. The LORD said to Moses, "Take the staff, and you and your brother Aaron gather the assembly together. Speak to that rock before their eyes and it will pour out its water. You will bring water out of the rock for the community so they and their livestock can drink". So Moses took the staff from the LORD's presence, just as he commanded him. He and Aaron gathered the assembly together in front of the rock and Moses said to them, "Listen, you rebels, must we bring you water out of this rock"? Then Moses *raised his arm and struck the rock twice with his staff.* Water gushed out, and the community and their livestock drank. But the LORD said to Moses and Aaron, "Because you did not trust in me enough to honor me as holy in the sight of the Israelites, you will not bring this community into the land I give them'. These were the waters of Meribah, where the Israelites quarreled with the LORD and where he was proved holy among them" (Numbers 20:2–13).

I have underlined the areas of the Unforgivable Sin build-up by severity in: 1) underlining and 2) underlining with italicize. Let me explain … when Moses arrogantly and pridefully said to the Israelites, "must we …", he did this in the face of God Almighty, blessed be He, who was invisibly standing by to perform the miracle. So, when Moses immediately followed through in his disobedience by striking the rock instead of speaking to it, noted above, he committed the Unforgivable Sin because of his self-pride – essentially, steeling God's glory to exalt himself as if he, Moses, performed the miracle, on his own. Moses' behavior in this act was a haughtiness that God hates … as it is written: "There are six things the LORD hates, seven that are detestable to him: haughty eyes …" (Proverbs 6:16-17). Because haughty eyes is the first thing God mentions of the list of seven things, make no mistake, the first one addressed here is the most severe of them all to Him. It is also important to remember here, this time at the rock where Moses committed this Unforgivable Sin was the second time God brought water out from it for the Israelites to drink. However, the first time Moses obeyed God's instructions perfectly and honored Him, feared Him, reverenced Him with love … as a good son shows his love for his Dad – in this way, God was supremely glorified through His servant Moses. This is how we get to feel and understand The Father's heart in this matter, by differentiating between the obedience vs. the disobedience to Him. Yes, God still favored his children who were complaining, and by His great mercies and grace and by His word, which is His bond – He performed the miracle for the Israelites (His weak sheep who He so jealously loved) and even though Moses disobeyed Him the second time. Irrevocably however, God's anger was slowly aroused over all the haughty moments in Moses' testimony, but it fully matured and was unleashed at this abominable committal by Moses; hence, God's explanation highlighted in green. If you are wondering, what were some other haughty moments leading up to this event? Moses out of quick-anger, as one example, had broken the tablets that The Father inscribed the ten commandments on, by throwing them out of rage and breaking them at the foot of a mountain. Yes, there was a reason why Moses got angry, but it became haughty when he failed to reverence God in His works where He inscribed, Himself, the ten commandments. God then had to re-inscribe the ten commandments later – redo His holy works on account of Moses' haughtiness. Remember, there are two distinct parts to this Unforgivable Sin, which are in short: 1) breaking faith, and 2) forfeiting God's holiness in His active presence. So, although Moses was quick-to-anger at times in God's sight throughout his lifetime, those acts alone were not unforgivable. It didn't become unforgiveable until Moses forfeited God's holiness in His active sight before all the Israelites. This arrogant, haughty, irrevocably abominable – self-pride demonstrated through a God-fearing person is the root cause of this Unforgivable Sin, in this first case by Moses, a servant of God. It is worth noting that this Unforgivable Sin has a build-up to it before becoming fully mature, but we will discuss that later in the book when we get into the seeds and their manifestations leading up to it.

# UNFORGIVABLE SIN'S CURSE

God revealed to me years ago when I first read about the story of Moses and the Israelites, that his Unforgivable Sin at the Rock of Meribah set a path of recurring curses generationally. In other words, from generation to generation leading up to this very moment, the sin Moses committed has falsely influenced people to this very day. So, I will explain it as The Holy Spirit revealed to me ...

When Moses committed this Unforgivable Sin, God's wrath did not fall upon Moses immediately. In fact, Moses continued to serve the Lord for quite some time without obvious punishment. Now, let me remind you of several kinds of sins in the Old Testament that were unforgivable with respect to a death sentence such as: adultery, murder in cold blood, and witchcraft. These sins today under the New Covenant, do not warrant unforgiveness. Conversely, now as a servant, active with The Holy Spirit, having broken faith and forfeiting God's holiness – this is when it is committed. Moses committed this first – defined by God Almighty, later Jesus would teach His disciples about it – warning them as He knew they would all betray Him at the cross, or in Judas' case, beforehand. More on that later ...

So, you might be thinking ... "what is the generational curse"? Because God chose to punish Moses much later in time, and to continue using him in the ministry to get the Israelites close to the promised land. However, Moses' influence from that day remained uncorrected ... at least, for a long period of time. As such, that influence propagated into idolatry – God's children placing a mortal man above Him, The Creator (violating the first commandment) – many to this day believe Jesus was a prophet, but that Moses has supremacy over Him. In fact, Jesus makes this revelation clear in the New Testament when He said to the Pharisees': "But do not think I will accuse you before the Father. Your accuser is Moses, on whom your hopes are set. If you believed Moses, you would believe me, for he wrote about me. But since you do not believe what he wrote, how are you going to believe what I say" (John 5:45–47)? This is a deep revelation about the scriptures, yet proving the Pharisees' hypocritical – focusing on law, and denouncing the coming of a New Covenant foretold through the widely known prophecy of the coming of The Messiah. This is referenced in the Books of Isaiah and Jeremiah in the Old Testament, as they are written: "For to us a child is born, to us a son is given, and the government will be on his shoulders. And he will be called Wonderful Counselor, Mighty God, Everlasting Father, Prince of Peace. Of the greatness of his government and peace there will be no end. He will reign on David's throne and over his kingdom, establishing and upholding it with justice and righteousness from that time on and forever. The zeal of the Lord Almighty will accomplish this" (Isaiah 9:6–7).

And then … "This is the covenant I will make with the people of Israel after that time," declares the Lord. "I will put my law in their minds and write it on their hearts. I will be their God, and they will be my people. No longer will they teach their neighbor, or say to one another, Know the Lord, because they will all know me, from the least of them to the greatest," declares the Lord. "For I will forgive their wickedness and will remember their sins no more" (Jeremiah 31:33–34). This too, was later cross-referenced in the New Testament: The Holy Spirit also testifies to us about this. First he says: "This is the covenant I will make with them after that time, says the Lord. I will put my laws in their hearts, and I will write them on their minds." Then he adds: "Their sins and lawless acts I will remember no more." And where these have been forgiven, sacrifice for sin is no longer necessary (Hebrews 10:15–18).

Therefore, the Pharisees' rejected scripture and The Messiah – making them a double hypocrite since they rejected Moses and the scriptures he authored, the prophecies of Isaiah and Jeremiah, and the truth in their faces by virtue of The Messiah in flesh and in their presence. In essence – this double hypocrisy is the rejection of Old and New Covenants. As such, the curse lives on. As I alluded to earlier in this book, God is revealing through this spirit-led teaching to combat and place a path forward for reconciling the truth in these End Times. Amazing! More on that later …

# ANOTHER OT EXAMPLE

Now let us take another look at this Unforgiveable Sin in the testimony of King Saul to sharpen our spiritual awareness and understanding – using what we've learned in Moses' testimony to reveal the sin-phases leading up to the Unforgiveable Sin in this next example.

Real quick … Who is King Saul? What was the timing of his Kingship relative to Moses' (establishing some sense of history and chronology)? By the time King Saul comes into play Biblically, who is David's predecessor. There was an estimated 460 years from the time Moses died and Joshua succeeded him as King (1390 BC) to the time Saul became King (930 BC). Again, this is provided merely to give some sense as to when the act is clearly committed again after Moses' death.

To summarize in a paraphrasing manner, prior to Saul becoming King, the Israelites became concerned that they had no appointed King like the other surrounding Kingdoms. In fact, the prophet Samuel intervened as interim leader to the Israelites, but as he grew older he appointed his son's to help lead … but because Samuel's sons were showing signs of unjustness, the Israelites complained and said to the prophet Samuel, "We want a King like the other nations." During this time, God Almighty, blessed be He, was disappointed with the Israelites because He was their King Himself, but the Israelites did not realize that as they had become stiff necked, yet again. In other words, forgetting their God who had saved them from the slavery of the Egyptians and the many miracles performed by Him through God's servant Moses. Yes, the curse revealed in the prior part of this book is evident here. Therefore, God spoke to His prophet Samuel and said: "Give them what they want." All this that is paraphrased can be corroborated with The Book of 1 Samuel, Chapter 8.

After some time had passed, Samuel anoints Saul according to God's command. As it is written: "Then Samuel took a flask of olive oil and poured it on Saul's head and kissed him, saying, 'Has not the LORD anointed you ruler over his inheritance'" (1 Samuel 10:1). Just after this anointing, the prophet Samuel prophesied over

Saul that the Spirit of the Lord would fall upon him and cause him to also prophesy. As it is written: "The Spirit of the LORD will come powerfully upon you, and you will prophesy with them; and you will be changed into a different person. Once these signs are fulfilled, do whatever your hand finds to do, for God is with you" (1 Samuel 10:6–7). These signs God foretold through His prophet Samuel were fulfilled the same day. As such, Saul is activated by The Holy Spirit with the gift of prophesy - very important we capture this significant moment in Saul's testimony. Then Saul was confirmed King.

Early in King Saul's reign, he would disobey God's instruction. King Saul would then be rebuked by the prophet Samuel and would be instructed that God has sought after another man who was after God's own heart. King Saul's disobedience would continue, in fact, throughout most of his 42-year reign as King. As the years would go by, and as God's newly elect-to-be would come into the picture, which was David, jealousy would soon set in with King Saul as David would demonstrate to be a mighty warrior. This is especially evident when the people of Israel would exalt David's efforts of killing the giant Philistine by the name of Goliath. As it is written: "When the men were returning home after David had killed the Philistine, the women came out from all the towns of Israel to meet King Saul with singing and dancing, with joyful songs and with timbrels and lyres. As they danced, they sang: 'Saul has slain his thousands, and David his tens of thousands'" (1 Samuel 18:6-7). The anger and jealousy of King Saul towards David would grow so intense that he would attempt to kill David multiple times. Fast forwarding through some of the story, next will venture into the depths of King Saul's committal of the Unforgivable Sin.

King Saul commits the Unforgivable Sin. As it is written: But the king said, "You will surely die, Ahimelek, you and your whole family." Then the king ordered the guards at his side: "Turn and kill the priests of the LORD, because they too have sided with David. They knew he was fleeing, yet they did not tell me. But the king's officials were unwilling to raise a hand to strike the priests of the

LORD." The king then ordered Doeg, "You turn and strike down the priests." 'So Doeg, the Edomite, turned and struck them down. That day he killed eighty-five men who wore the linen ephod. He also put to the sword Nob, the town of the priests, with its men and women, its children and infants, and its cattle, donkeys and sheep' (1 Samuel 22:16 – 19). So we see here how the arrogance of King Saul would explode to a level where he completely disregards God Almighty and in His presence Saul would command his servants to kill "the Lord's priests" – blaspheming The Holy Spirit as it was spoken and then carried out – breaking faith with God and forfeiting God's holiness in the sight of many men and in the sight of God Almighty. Next, will synoptically break this event down further ...

So, we learned that King Saul started off as a God-fearing man, as he would reverence God. As it is written: "But Saul said, 'No one will be put to death today, for this day the LORD has rescued Israel.' Then Samuel said to the people, 'Come, let us go to Gilgal and there renew the kingship.' So all the people went to Gilgal and made Saul king in the presence of the LORD. There they sacrificed fellowship offerings before the LORD, and Saul and all the Israelites held a great celebration" (1 Samuel 11:13–15).

In addition to being God-fearing, King Saul was activated by The Holy Spirit with the gift of prophesy. This gift and all the gifts of The Holy Spirit according to the Bible are manifestations of God's holiness, and it is through fellowship with The Holy Spirit that the gifts manifest. Therefore, all three components that characterize the person who commits this Unforgivable Sin are represented here in King Saul's testimony.

Unlike in Moses' case, God separated from King Saul permanently once he committed the Unforgivable Sin. King Saul would have the audacity to consult a medium for guidance and direction as his reign was coming to an end and as tensions would rise among the Philistines ... as terror consumed his heart – this can be corroborated in The Book of 1 Samuel, Chapter 28. Fast forward a little after that discourse, King Saul would commit suicide – by plunging his own sword through his body by falling on it – a disgraceful death. Spiritually, the sword represents God and His holy scriptures, as the Word of God is our greatest weapon for spiritual warfare. So spiritually King Saul died by killing himself most disgracefully – symbolically with God's holiness, yet physically with a sharp instrument.

# MOSES' OUTCOME

Make no mistake, Father God, blessed be He, can make any exceptions to the rule of law He pleases … this is a mysterious character of His holiness no human will fully understand. As it is written: "For my thoughts are not your thoughts, neither are your ways my ways," declares the LORD. "As the heavens are higher than the earth, so are my ways higher than your ways and my thoughts than your thoughts" (Isaiah 55:8–9). On Moses' account, although we learn from scriptures that he was the first man of God who betrays God in an unforgiving way that Jesus makes known in the New Testament as Blaspheme against The Holy Spirit. Thus, it is through other Holy Scriptures, 3 Enoch, we fully understand spiritually what happened to Moses, because without its revelation on account of Moses, you would likely be left wondering what happened to him, as the common Bible mentions Moses was commanded by God to die on Mount Nebo. It also states that his grave was never found (ref. Deuteronomy Ch. 34), and in the New Testament it states that Satan fought with Michael the archangel over Moses' body (ref. Jude 1). Yet again in the New Testament we learn that Moses fellowshipped with Jesus during His transfiguration prior to Him being captured to be crucified (ref. Matthew Ch. 17). So, what does all this mean, especially if Moses' committed the Unforgivable Sin?

As I mentioned earlier, God The Father, can make any exception He pleases. Yes, Moses committed the Unforgivable Sin by definition – as he broke faith and forfeited God's holiness; however, unlike all other scriptural accounts, we learn that God continued to use Moses after the comital to help get the Israelites close to the promised land. God made it clear to His servant Moses, that he would not enter the promised land, and that he would only get to see it from a distance. Regardless, this is unique compared to all other committed scriptural accounts, as the servants would more rapidly die with God being separated from them … conversely, God never separated from His servant Moses. Interesting! The term, "unforgivable", suggests that such a sin is so severe that would lead to eternal punishment, also referred to as Hades. Yet, Moses was commanded to die whether against his own will as God so decreed it, and even though the scriptures make it clear that Moses was in good health. So, this was a severe consequence to Moses' committal of the Unforgivable Sin, but God made an exception. Let me explain …

Unlike any other scriptural account of a servant of God who commits this Unforgivable Sin, Moses was given an opportunity to repent when his soul ascended into heaven. It is fascinating that there is a God-breathed written account of what happened to Moses' soul and how the angelic hosts responded. Let us get excited as we dive into the Holy Waters of 3 Enoch!

## GOD'S JUDGEMENT TO MOSES

As mentioned in the book 3 Enoch, The Hebrew Book, chapter 15-B and versus 2–5 (Schnieders, Paul C., 2012): "And when Moses ascended on high, he fasted 121 fasts, till the habitations of the chasmal were opened to him; and he (B: version) saw the heart of the heart of the Lion and he saw the innumerable companies of the hosts around about him. And they desired to burn him. But Moses prayed for mercy, first for Israel and after that for himself: and He who sitteth on the Merkaba opened the widows that are above the heads of the Kerubim. And a host of 1800 advocates – and the Prince of the Presence, Metatron, with them – went forth to meet Moses. And they took the prayers of Israel and put them as a crown on the head of the Holy One, blessed be He. And they said (Deut. 6:4): 'Hear, O Israel; the Lord our God is one Lord' and their face shone and rejoiced over Shekina and they said to Metatron: 'What are these? And to whom do they give all this honor and glory'? And they answered: 'To the Glorious Lord of Israel.' And they spake: 'Hear, O Israel: the Lord, our God, is one Lord. To whom shall be given abundance of honor and majesty but to Thee YHWH, the Divine Majesty, the King, living and eternal'. In that moment spake Akatriel Yah Yehod Sebaoth and said to Metatron, the Prince of the Presence: 'Let no prayer that he prayeth before me return (to him) void. Hear thou his prayer and fulfill his desire whether (it be) great or small'. Forthwith Metatron, the Prince of the Presence, said to Moses: 'Son of Amram! Fear not, for now God delights in thee, and ask thou thy desire of the Glory and Majesty. For thy face shines from one end of the world to the other'. But Moses answered him: '(I fear) lest I bring guiltiness upon myself.' Metatron said to him: 'Receive the letters of the oath, in (by) which there is no breaking the covenant' (which precludes any breach of the covenant)".

So, we see the soul of Moses was preserved for a length of time after his flesh died to the earth and was eventually acquitted. This happens to be the only written scriptural account the author has been spiritually made aware of where a man of God whose soul was forgiven for what Jesus calls the Unforgiveable Sin. Again, we need not understand God's rationale – He can make any exception He pleases. From God's verdict as mentioned in Enoch 3, we can understand why the angelic hosts of heaven were anticipating the burning of Moses' soul – as they were aware of the sin he committed. Then we see this struggle between Michael the archangel and Satan because God chose to vindicate Moses after receiving his prayers for the people of Israel and himself – important to understand, this took place in the realm of heaven with Moses' soul before final judgement had taken place (theologically known as 'purgatory'). We learned from 3 Enoch Moses soul was given 121 fasts before his prayers reached God before His final judgement to Moses. This would also explain the fight of Moses body between Michael and Satan since

Moses soul was given time to repent while in Heaven – scripture does not teach this being a common practice of God. Important to realize, both the Holy Hosts of Heaven and the evil one, Satan, were in agreement before God's final judgement. The fight for Moses' body is understandable when we know the process permitted here on Moses' behalf. All that said, regardless of popular beliefs ... God Almighty always has the final say!

As we come to an end here, and as I mentioned in the introduction of the book, I feel led by Holy Spirit to make a sharp warning about God's grace. Yes, He is merciful, gracious, compassionate, long-suffering, patient, slow to anger, just, perfect - this list goes on ... We cannot allow the process of Moses to somehow cause us in the World to flirt or take for granted God's grace. Please! Don't do that! Moses was a servant of God ... did many exploits for Him and His Son Jesus ... true repentance is a turning away from a prior lifestyle. As the author (widely believed to be Apostle Paul) would teach us now under the New Covenant – "Let us then approach God's throne of grace with confidence, so that we may receive mercy and find grace to help us in our time of need" (Hebrews 4:16). Moses, although a servant of the Most High God, did not approach God's throne of grace boldly, but seemingly cowardly and fearfully in an unsure way. So, I warn us all, do not take God's grace in vain. Let's learn to honor and respect and reverence God's grace.

# HEART OF JESUS

Now that we understand the heart of the Father, we now learn about the heart of His son, Jesus, with respect to the Unforgivable Sin. There is a shift between how the Father and Jesus focus on this sin – in essence, the Father focused on the act as referred to in the Old Testament, whereas Jesus focuses on the consequence in the New Testament. What do I mean? We learned that in Moses' testimony God mentioned to the effect: "Since you (Moses) did not uphold My holiness and you broke faith with Me, you will not enter the promised land." Therefore, God in this example focused on the act of Moses where he committed the Unforgivable Sin. Jesus, however, focused on the consequence as He was teaching His disciples: "And so I tell you, every kind of sin and slander can be forgiven, but blasphemy against the Spirit will not be forgiven" (Matthew 12:31). Jesus was teaching His disciples during this discourse after they had witnessed Jesus driving out an evil spirit (and healing the man's blindness and muteness) and where the Pharisees were making the claim that Jesus was only able to drive out the evil spirit by being a part of the evil spirit, to paraphrase. The key here is even more than Jesus addressing the Pharisees by them saying to the effect: "How can Satan drive out Satan", knowing that their hearts were full of falsehood and hypocrisy because other Jews had also been casting evil spirits out of others. Jesus was teaching that a kingdom divided cannot stand. This was a serious teaching primarily for Jesus' disciples, as He was soon to die, be raised from the dead, and then sit at the right hand of His Father in heaven. When this was to happen, Jesus was preparing His twelve disciples that there will come a time when He would later send His Holy Spirit to invisibly govern them and to have them perform the same miraculous works as Jesus performed, and to reverence The Holy Spirit, so as not to forfeit His holiness and break faith with Him. See, it is in the active presence of The Holy Spirit where He can be blasphemed. Therefore, contrary to many professing Christian ministers and teachers and their belief in this matter, an unbeliever cannot commit this Unforgivable Sin. You must know The Holy Spirit, commune with Him, fellowship with Him, have an intimate relationship with Him to be in His active presence where you could forfeit His holiness and break faith with Him. God the Father addressed this issue directly with His servant the prophet Ezekiel when He spoke: "Therefore, son of man, speak to the people of Israel and say to them, 'This is what the Sovereign LORD says: In this also your ancestors blasphemed me by being unfaithful to me'" (Ezekiel 20:27). Although many mean well, it is false teaching when Christians say that the Unforgivable Sin cannot be committed by Christians. The Bible teaches us in spirit that it is only by Christians who fellowship and believe in the invisible Holy Spirit where this sin can be committed. In other words, a person who is ignorant of The Holy Spirit cannot sin against Him, as it is written: "It is impossible for those who have once been enlightened, who have tasted the heavenly gift, who have shared in the Holy Spirit, who have tasted the goodness of the word of God and the powers of the coming age and who have fallen away, to be brought back to repentance. To their loss they are crucifying the Son of God all over again and subjecting him to public disgrace" (Hebrews 6:4-6). This scripture found in The Book of Hebrews is saying, in essence, that this sin is so severe that it is impossible to be redeemed through repentance; thus, deemed unforgivable as Jesus taught His disciples when you come to know The Holy Spirit. This scripture also teaches that the Unforgivable Sin is committed by those who have: "tasted the heavenly gift" – "shared in the Holy Spirit" – "tasted the goodness of the word of God." My dear brothers and sisters, far and near, among the world of unbelief and those a part of the Body of Christ – with great love I tell you - the Unforgivable Sin cannot be committed out of ignorance. Ignorance of the testimony of Jesus Christ, His distributed power of The Holy Spirit by the favor of God The Father who justifies His Son is not unforgivable – it's unbelief. Unbelief is forgivable.

Let's go back to the story where Jesus was teaching His disciples in the presence of the Pharisees where they were making the claim about how Jesus cast out the evil spirit. To be exact and as it is written: " ...It is only by Beelzebul, the prince of demons, that this fellow drives out demons" (Matthew 12:24). Clearly the Pharisees in this example were calling Jesus, the son of God, "prince of demons". Yes, this was blasphemous ... this is literally a name calling that was blasphemous against the name of Jesus, but not against The Holy Spirit. I have seen some false teaching on this that absolutely rocks me to the core of my being that basically is opposite of what scriptures represent, especially since Jesus clearly explains as follows: "Anyone who speaks a word against the Son of Man will be forgiven, but anyone who speaks against the Holy Spirit will not be forgiven, either in this age or in the age to come" (Matthew 12:32). The Pharisees did not know The Holy Spirit, so how could they have blasphemed Him (referring to the false teaching in this generation)? Thus, they directed their name calling towards Jesus, who in their presence healed the man who had an evil spirit, and yes, Jesus did it by the power of the invisible Holy Spirit, but the name calling was towards Jesus Himself. So, to answer the question, the Pharisees didn't blaspheme The Holy Spirit, and they themselves could even be forgiven – make no mistake, Jesus was deeply concerned for the Pharisees as well as the rest of the people in the World. Yes, the Pharisees were known to be hypocrites, and their name Pharisee is widely used in theology to represent hypocrisy in general – but make no mistake, hypocrisy is forgivable. If it were not, me, myself and I would be dead and cast to Hades forever, but God saved me in 2012 after having been a big hypocrite. Hallelujah! But in this case, the true teaching was for the disciples to learn that what they will come to know through their fellowship with The Holy Spirit (invisibly), that they shall always reverence The Holy Spirit – because it will be Him who performs the signs, miracles and wonders through the disciples' yielded vessels as Jesus was teaching, and that you all shall not speak like the Pharisees in this manner when you yourselves come to know The Holy Spirit whom I (meaning Jesus) send to you all. This was essentially a warning that when the disciples come to know The Holy Spirit, it would be the Unforgivable Sin should they speak arrogantly like the Pharisees by forfeiting God's holiness (Holy Spirit) and breaking faith with Him. I feel deeply convicted to coin and press this issue into the hearts of my dear brothers' and sisters' who are unsure about this Unforgivable Sin, perhaps you reading this ... for the first time ... you have learned in spirit correctly as even The Holy Spirit bears witness to this truth within us now. Next, we'll investigate the New Testament for some examples of those who blasphemed against The Holy Spirit and committed the Unforgivable Sin.

## JUDAS ONE OF THE TWELVE DISCIPLES

In this example, we will investigate the testimony of Judas who was one of the original twelve disciples of Jesus and how he committed the Unforgivable Sin. However, this example will bring attention to the seed first. Yes, there is a spiritual seed that precedes the full-blown committal of the Unforgivable Sin ... the seed is the lukewarm spirit. You may be thinking: what is the lukewarm spirit? Lukewarm is the mixture of Christianity (hot) and idolatry (cold) – it is a demonic blend of perceived good and evil - the perceived love of Jesus mixed with the love of money. Thus, like the Unforgivable Sin, lukewarm, when fully mature, is committed before blaspheming against The Holy Spirit, but once committed the faulted soul without repentance is near the committal of the Unforgivable Sin. Important to know here as well, that the sin of being lukewarm cannot be committed without knowing and testifying to the testimony of Jesus and activated by His Holy Spirit – it cannot be committed under the ignorance of Jesus' testimony. Jesus says this about the lukewarm spirit in The Book of Revelation as He was addressing the church angel (pastor) of Laodicea: "I know your deeds, that you are neither cold nor hot. I wish you were either one or the other! So, because you are lukewarm—neither hot nor cold—I am about to spit you out of my mouth. You say, 'I am rich; I have acquired wealth and do not need a thing.' But you do not realize that you are wretched, pitiful, poor, blind and naked" (Versus 3:15–17). Therefore, following will provide a spiritual synopsis gleaning from the life of Judas, detailing how the seed of the lukewarm spirit is fully matured, then followed by the committal of blaspheming against The Holy Spirit – which soon after led to Judas committing suicide (like King Saul in the Old Testament) because of the insurmountable weight of guilt and disgrace upon his irrevocably haunted soul.

Judas before he betrays Jesus, was a part of Jesus' ministry. In fact, Jesus launched His disciples and charged them to go into Israel, this included Judas. As it is written: "Jesus called his twelve disciples to him and gave them authority to drive out impure spirits and to heal every disease and sickness" (Matthew 10:1). Then Jesus instructed them all as follows: "Do not go among the Gentiles or enter any town of the Samaritans. Go rather to the lost sheep of Israel. As you go, proclaim this message: 'The kingdom of heaven has come near.' Heal the sick, raise the dead, cleanse those who have leprosy, drive out demons. Freely you have received; freely give" (Matthew 10:5–8). As we learned here in the Gospel of Matthew, Jesus gave His disciples spiritual authority to perform the noted works – to bless the lost sheep of Israel. This authority that Jesus speaks of comes by His Holy Spirit – Jesus essentially charged them during this mission with the power of The Holy Spirit - activated them – as it is only by The Holy Spirit that He "drive out demons" and evil spirits in Jesus' name. Therefore, Judas was clearly activated with Holy Spirit by the favor of The Father in Heaven upon the request of His son Jesus, blessed be He and He and He as One Triune God. This is a unique way of respecting the triune – One God represented in three characters – Father, Son and Holy Spirit. All in perfect unity here.

Jesus predicts the betrayal that would be acted out by Judas. This betrayal was also prophesied by the Old Testament prophets to fully substantiate the truth of all God-breathed scriptures (Old and New Testaments) - irrefutably. This prophetic truth is referred to in The Book of Acts chapter 1 verse 20, but it is referring to The Book of Psalms chapter 69 verses 25-28 as follows: "May their place be deserted; let there be no one to dwell in their tents. For they persecute those you wound and talk about the pain of those you hurt. Charge them with crime upon crime; do not let them share in your salvation. May they be blotted out of the book of life and not be listed with the righteous" (Biblegateway.com, 2011).

As the Gospels detail, Judas makes an agreement with the hypocritical chief priests, as it is written: "Then one of the Twelve— the one called Judas Iscariot—went to the chief priests and asked, "What are you willing to give me if I deliver him over to you?" So they counted out for him thirty pieces of silver. From then on Judas watched for an opportunity to hand him over" (Matthew 26:14–16). This became the act of the lukewarm sin that Judas committed just before committing the Unforgivable Sin – in other words, this was the seed to blaspheme against The Holy Spirit. Then shortly after, Jesus at the Last Supper predicts Judas' unforgivable betrayal, as it is written: " …The one who has dipped his hand into the bowl with me will betray me. The Son of Man will go just as it is written about him. But woe to that man who betrays the Son of Man! It would be better for him if he had not been born" (Matthew 26:14 – 16). Yes, this is Jesus speaking, and make no mistake – Jesus was foretelling the Hades -destined condemnation here so that all His disciples would come to know how evil and unpardonable this act was going to be that their fellow brother in The Body of Christ, Judas, was about to commit.

Judas commits the Unforgivable Sin. After the supper, Jesus with His disciples go to a place called Gethsemane to pray as Jesus was deeply distressed. It was there where Jesus had instructed His disciples to keep watch and to not fall asleep, yet they did anyways, multiple times. "Then he returned to the disciples and said to them, 'Are you still sleeping and resting? Look, the hour has come, and the Son of Man is delivered into the hands of sinners. Rise! Let us go! Here comes my betrayer'" (Matthew 26:45–46). Then, as it is written: "While he was still speaking, Judas, one of the Twelve, arrived. With him was a large crowd armed with swords and clubs, sent from the chief priests and the elders of the people. Now the betrayer had arranged a signal with them: 'The one I kiss is the man; arrest him.' Going at once to Jesus, Judas said, 'Greetings, Rabbi!' and kissed him" (Matthew 26:47–49). The kiss of betrayal was the Unforgivable Sin that blasphemed against The Holy Spirit. This was breaking faith and forfeiting of God's holiness, as Jesus was the distributor of God's Holy Spirit to His disciples, as they were performing the works Jesus had commissioned them to with spiritual authority – under the unction of The Holy Spirit. This was a direct forfeiting of God The Father's New Covenant and gift through His son Jesus – whom by the favor of the Father on His son's behalf, where Judas performed signs, miracles, and wonders as a vessel. It was The Holy Spirit through Judas' vessel that was casting out demons … it was The Holy Spirit that was raising the dead … it was The Holy Spirit that cleansed the lepers … all in the name of Jesus of Nazareth.

Unlike Moses or King Saul, the irrevocable guilt and shame and disgrace quickly led Judas to commit suicide. If you recall, Moses and King Saul were not charged with death quickly after their committals of the Unforgivable Sins – it had taken some time before they finally died of their flesh. Nonetheless, what had happened to Judas was done to fulfill scriptures – both Old and New Testaments … as it is written: "With the payment he received for his wickedness, Judas bought a field; there he fell headlong, his body burst open and all his intestines spilled out. Everyone in Jerusalem heard about this, so they called that field in their language Akeldama, that is, Field of Blood. 'For,' said Peter, 'it is written in the Book of Psalms':

'May his place be deserted; let there be no one to dwell in it,' and, 'May another take his place of leadership'" (Acts 1:18–20). Thus,

Judas hung himself – dying disgracefully and condemned to Hades for all eternity in the manner foretold. Remember, Jesus said: "It would be better for him if he had not been born." In other words, unforgivable and condemned to eternal death ... Hades became the inheritance of Judas' soul. Thus, Jesus' disciples reconfirmed also just before replacing Judas, as it is written: " ...to take over this apostolic ministry, which Judas left to go where he belongs" (Acts 1:25).

# ANANIAS AND SAPPHIRA THE CHURCH COUPLE

The next example of the Unforgivable Sin, is the first written account after Jesus died on the cross and returned to the heavenlies, as committed by a church couple Ananias and his wife Sapphira. We find this written account in The Book of Acts, chapter 5. Leading to this account in chapter 4 we learn that the early Christian churches lead by the Lord's apostles were strengthening in spirit and increasing in numbers in a harmonious and unified way, as it is written: "All the believers were one in heart and mind. No one claimed that any of their possessions was their own, but they shared everything they had. With great power the apostles continued to testify to the resurrection of the Lord Jesus. And God's grace was so powerfully at work in them all that there were no needy persons among them. For from time to time those who owned land or houses sold them, brought the money from the sales and put it at the apostles' feet, and it was distributed to anyone who had need" (Acts 4:32–35). This noteworthy Christian movement included the couple Ananias and Sapphira; however, they did not hold up to the same standards established by the church, and committed a wicked, unpardonable act ...

In chapter 5 of The Book of Acts we learn that Ananias and Sapphira sold their belongings, but unlike their church brothers and sisters based on a mutual agreement and instead of providing all their earned money from their sale, they kept a portion of the money for themselves. This breeched the covenant of the church, and in the sight of the Lord. When first confronted by Peter, Ananias lied about his wickedness without speaking a word … then immediately dropped dead. Some three hours later, his wife Sapphira was confronted and lied to Peter as well without speaking a word, and she too died immediately. Now remember, the power of the Holy Spirit was heavily upon the Lord's apostles, so when this couple lied to the church, namely Peter, they lied to God as His great power was with him and the other apostles. This great power was The Holy Spirit. Therefore, Ananias and his wife Sapphira blasphemed against The Holy Spirit when they lied without returning to reverence and thus holding to their story they formed together, as one flesh they united in wickedness and as one flesh they perished disgracefully – like Judas, their punishment was immediate death of their flesh and likely Hades fire for all eternity. Peter's last words to Sapphira before her death: "How could you conspire to test the Spirit of the Lord? Listen! The feet of the men who buried your husband are at the door, and they will carry you out also" (Acts 5:9).

# KING HEROD THE KING OF JUDAEA

The last example found in The Book of Acts, chapter 12, is the committal of the Unforgivable Sin carried out by King Herod Agrippa. Before his unforgivable act is foretold hereof, it is important to share some of his testimony and family lineage. King Herod Agrippa was fourth generation from Herod the Great, who was also a king. Herod the Great was the king of Judaea, who in Jesus' time as an infant plotted to have baby Jesus killed. To his demise, Herod the Great died shortly after his order to have all young boys two years of age and younger killed. Agrippa's great, great, great grandfather Herod the Great also blasphemed against The Holy Spirit when knowingly attempting to kill the Messiah, and specifically mentioned himself: "the Messiah." Knowing in Jewish customs and religion the word 'Messiah' means: "God's anointed." Interestingly, his death was predicted by the angel helping to protect Jesus' family when ordered to escape to Egypt. Thus, Herod the Great's death came to pass. In the same manner King Saul in the Old Testament blasphemed against The Holy Spirit by saying: "Kill the Lord's priests" – Herod the Great did as well when knowingly confessing his plot to kill "The Messiah." These accounts can be corroborated in The Book of Matthew, chapter 2. I have chosen not to expound on this account in detail, but enough to bring greater understanding as to Agrippa's family lineage and blasphemous history. Now, let us keenly focus our attention on the accounts in The Book of Acts, regarding King Herod Agrippa.

There is a lot of Jewish literature that describes Herod Agrippa's accounts in detail, even more detail than The Book of Acts, so I will paraphrase some of which found in The Book of Josephus, volume 4. Before anointed king of Judaea, Agrippa was imprisoned. There was a day an angel came to speak to a guardsman and have him translate what the angel said to Agrippa. In short, the angel's (in the form of an owl) message to Agrippa was to know he would be divinely provided for the rest of his years and seated as king of Judaea and live happily until his death. Just before his death he would see the angel again. Like his great, great, great grandfather Herod the Great, his death was predicted.

After some time had passed, when established as the highest seat of power, as the angel foretold, King Herod Agrippa publicly spoke to the people of Judaea. As it is written: "On the appointed day Herod, wearing his royal robes, sat on his throne and delivered a public address to the people. They shouted, 'This is the voice of a god, not of a man.' Immediately, because Herod did not give praise to God, an angel of the Lord struck him down, and he was eaten by worms and died" (Acts 12:21–23). As you may recall learning about earlier in the teaching, Moses committed a similar act that led to his committal of the Unforgivable Sin. As Moses at the rock of Meribah the second time, stole God's glory by making the miracle in front of the Israelites as though he and his brother Aaron performed it when the water came out from the rock, so did King Herod Agrippa by not correcting the persons who called him, in essence, "a god", when delivering his speech. This had the same appearance as what happened with Moses; however, the death of King Herod Agrippa ensued much faster as the grace of God had been quickened to preserve the church of Christ. More on the quickening of God's grace, as a response to committing the Unforgivable Sin under the New Covenant later in the book.

Closing exhortation with respect to the 'Heart of Jesus'. The death of our Savior – Jesus Christ – once valued and realized as to the immensity of the grace of His sacrifice for all mankind, which we as humans cannot fathom. His longsuffering blesses us. We realize once the supernatural testimony of Jesus is made real to our conscience, spirit and soul that His grace is precious and deserving of supreme reverence and respect. His Holy Spirit is our greatest gift to us as a byproduct of salvation, as His Spirit guides us in all areas of life when born again in Christ our Savior (first born of flesh and blood, but secondarily by spirit in our belief in Jesus which is justified through faith). Therefore, being born again and then forfeiting God's holiness, and utterly devaluing the sacrifice of the Father in Heaven by giving of His only begotten son for us, the world and available to all mankind in it - and the ultimate sacrifice He made to be dismissed in His sight with utter arrogance and irreverence ... this is total destruction of the soul. As it is further coined in scripture: "How much more severely do you think someone deserves to be punished who has trampled the Son of God underfoot, who has treated as an unholy thing the blood of the covenant that sanctified them, and who has insulted the Spirit of grace" (Hebrews 10:29)? See, The Holy Spirit is also representative of God's grace, as we see here in Hebrews it refers to it as "Spirit of grace". This grace is a holy covering ... a grace that was provided for even those of us who didn't even know it ... so when we come into the knowledge of it, let us be encouraged to preserve it and protect it in our hearts so as not to become so irreverent we blaspheme Him as we mature in our works of Jesus' teachings.

# MERCY AND GRACE
# QUICKENED

It is fascinating to know, that God's mercy and grace was quickened in the New Testament compared to the Old Testament accounts, regarding the Unforgiveable Sin and its due punishment. In fact, it is more fascinating that this quickening was even foreshadowed in the Old Testament too ... as it is written: "As he went on his way, a lion met him on the road and killed him, and his body was left lying on the road, with both the donkey and the lion standing beside it" (1 Kings 13:24). I will explain this quickening in more detail ...

## OLD TESTAMENT ACCOUNTS

We learned in this book from the Holy Scriptures that when Moses committed this Unforgivable Sin his punishment didn't ensue until much later in time. God still used Moses after his committal of this sin to lead the Israelites close to "The promised land". After much time had passed, and just prior to the Israelites entering the promised land, God then commanded Moses' death on the top of Mount Nebo. We see here in this example in the Old Testament that God's rath was not unleashed until much service and time had passed after Moses' committed this Unforgivable Sin. In fact, we learned from the scriptures that Moses' brother Aaron died before Moses, as the Unforgiveable Sin was committed by both Moses and his brother Aaron … but on the account of Moses, his punishment didn't happen right away. Another fact, Moses wrote most of the Book of Deuteronomy after the committal.

One may ask: why did Aaron die first? I pointed out in this book previously that the seed leading to the Unforgivable Sin is the lukewarm spirit. Since Aaron was the High Priest, he had a leading role in the church ministry to uphold the standards God indoctrinated through His laws to Moses and the Jewish Israelites. When Aaron forged a golden calf shortly after Moses went to be alone with God at the top of Mount Sinai, which took place way before Moses taking the lead to committing the Unforgivable Sin at the rock of Meribah the second time during their travels, he committed the act of being lukewarm. Aaron, the High Priest, majorly backslid from God and His commands by committing the lukewarm act twice, and as Moses' accomplice for the committal of the Unforgivable Sin, since he did not immediately rebuke Moses when he said the very words and actions that followed those empty words that broke faith with God and forfeited His holiness in the sight of both God and the Israelites. For these reasons Aaron was slated to die before Moses according to the will of God The Father.

Also, we glean from the scriptures of Moses' written account of repentance found in Psalm 106 versus 32 and 33: "By the waters of Meribah they angered the LORD, and trouble came to Moses because of them; for they rebelled against the Spirit of God, and rash words came from Moses' lips". To be clear, Psalm 106 in its entirety is the written account of Moses' repentance unto the Lord. Because Moses was the first to commit the sin of its kind, we learned that God made an exception for Moses – both from The Book of 3 Enoch where God forgave Moses' soul and acquitted him and also in the New Testament where we find Moses and Elijah both fellowshipping with Jesus during His transfiguration prior to His crucifixion. As such, we learn that God spared Moses' soul, but we do not know that as fact for his brother Aaron. In either case, God's punishment was not immediate in this Old Testament account of Moses and Aaron. However, Aaron's death on top of Mount Hor came much sooner than Moses' on Mount Nebo as it is written: "At Mount Hor, near the border of Edom, the LORD said to Moses and Aaron, 'Aaron will be gathered to his people. He will not enter the land I give the Israelites, because both of you rebelled against my command at the waters of Meribah' " (Numbers 20:23-24).

Similarly, we learn that in the next written account of the committal of the Unforgivable Sin was by King Saul, David's predecessor. This account is found in 1 Samuel chapter 22 verses 17 through 19: "Then the king ordered the guards at his side: 'Turn and kill the priests of the LORD, because they too have sided with David. They knew he was fleeing, yet they did not tell me.' But the king's officials were unwilling to raise a hand to strike the priests of the LORD. The king then ordered Doeg, 'You turn and strike down the priests.' So Doeg the Edomite turned and struck them down. That day he killed eighty-five men who wore the linen ephod. He also put to the sword Nob, the town of the priests, with its men and women, its children and infants, and its cattle, donkeys and sheep." Thus, in this account King Saul's punishment was not immediate. In fact, we learn by these scriptures found in 1 Samuel that King Saul continued to attempt to ambush and kill David, God's anointed. Moses spoke by The Spirit of God when he said: "Do not touch my anointed ones; do my prophets no harm" (Psalm 105:15). Yet knowingly King Saul continuously rebelled in the sight of the Lord – surely he knew what he was doing so arrogantly ... so haughtily. It wasn't until King Saul's unsuccessful attempts to ambush David, where in 1 Samuel chapter 31 King Saul committed suicide by purposefully falling on his own sword – the most despicable and spiritually disgraceful death – death eternal! Nonetheless, God's rath was not immediate, but sooner the response time compared to Moses' account. This changes drastically as we venture into the New Testament accounts next.

# NEW TESTAMENT ACCOUNTS

In the New Testament, we learned that Judas Iscariot (one of the twelve original disciples of Jesus) committed this Unforgivable Sin first during Jesus' ministry, as King Herod committed it first in New Testament written accounts when Jesus was just a baby, but for this example we will focus on Judas the betrayer. As we learned earlier in this book and from the Gospels of Matthew chapter 26, Mark chapter 14, Luke chapter 22 and John chapter 18 Judas commits the Unforgivable Sin. Then in the Gospel of Matthew we learn that Judas the next morning commits suicide by hanging himself after being overwhelmed with guilt (ref. Matthew 27:5) – this was also to fulfill Old Testament prophecy through the prophet Jeremiah (ref. Jeremiah chapters 31 & 32). This account in the New Testament demonstrates God's grace performed this punishment in less than a day later of Judas committing the Unforgivable Sin. This coins the quickening of God's divine rath compared to the Old Testament accounts with respect to the committal of the Unforgivable Sin. Be that as it may, post resurrection of Jesus with respect to the accounts of the Unforgivable Sin, God's gracious rath is even quicker. Let us evaluate …

After the four Gospels: Matthew – Mark – Luke – John, the next written account of the committal of the Unforgivable Sin is found in The Book of Acts in the fifth chapter with the church couple, Ananias and Sapphira. Another excellent example of the progression of sins leading up to their joint committal of the Unforgivable Sin. So to paraphrase, we learn that the church of the apostles of Jesus were just activated with the anointing of The Holy Spirit baptism, as the Day of Pentecost which was prophesied even in the Old Testament (ref. Isaiah 44:3 and again in Joel 2:28), that the Holy Spirit would be poured out upon all flesh – this later was confirmed by Jesus, as it is written: "But very truly I tell you, it is for your good that I am going away. Unless I go away, the Advocate will not come to you; but if I go, I will send him to you" (John 16:7). Therefore, the apostles being fully activated with the Holy Spirit where this Unforgivable Sin is committed in the Book of Acts, we learn that Ananias, the husband, and his wife, Sapphira, first commit the sin of lukewarm which we learn in this book is the "seed" of the Unforgiveable Sin. Because as One Flesh they agreed to steal money from the church, they committed church-idolatry (lukewarm), but when confronted by Apostle Peter they both lied in the Holy presence of the Spirit of the Lord; thus, committing the Unforgivable Sin. In this written account, we learn that once the lie was committed from Ananias and Sapphira's hearts, God immediately gave up their Ghost and caused them to die. Although they died at separate times, they both died immediately after lying in the active presence of God (The Holy Spirit) – first Ananias the husband and then several hours later Sapphira his wife. We see here in this example, the grace of God acted immediately – so post resurrection of Jesus we see the holy wrath of God is now instantaneous.

In like manner as Ananias and Sapphira, King Herod Agrippa was the next written account of having committed the Unforgivable Sin post resurrection of Jesus. In this written account also found in the Boof of Acts chapter 12, we learn that similarly to Moses' committal and to paraphrase, King Herod Agrippa delivered a public address to the multitude and when voices from the crowd shouted: "This is the voice of a god, not of man" (Acts 12:22), God had his angel from Heaven immediately strike him, where shortly afterwards would be eaten by worms and died – although his death was not immediate, God's holy rath struck King Herod immediately, causing him to suffer a torturous death. Ironically, in some Jewish literature found in the Book of Josephus, which we learned in prior chapters of this book, that King Herod Agrippa's lavish life and death were predicted by the angel of God (in the form of an owl). We see common linkage between the language used – this is unique in the sense that God uses an angel as both messenger and death-deliverer to bless and punish King Herod Agrippa. In this account, you need both the Book of Acts and Josephus to fully substantiate these facts. Regardless, we learn God's wrath was instant in this account as it was with Ananias and Sapphira in the prior account.

# WHY THE QUICKENING OF GOD'S RATH?

By now you might be wondering, why? Why is the quickening of God's rath regarding the Unforgivable Sin referred to as "God's grace" and "His mercy" and "His holiness" if it is a result of someone's or multiple people's eternal death … yes, eternal death. Why? The Spirt of the Lord shared with me that the accounts of the Unforgivable Sin committed in the New Testament and the reasoning behind His quickened rath, to paraphrase: His punishment is merciful and gracious to help protect and preserve His church as His bride. His church is vast, extends beyond all countries – goes to and extends to all four corners of the world, since the church is His accumulated children of all the earth – those resting, those alive today, and those to come in the future, before His second coming. Yes, for those who don't know, Jesus is coming again to dwell on the earth with His saints for a thousand years, but He is not coming to save but to judge the earth as the Lion of Judah and King of kings at that time (ref. Revelation chapter 20). These written accounts in the New Testament help us know, Jesus' true disciples, that the closer we get to know Him and the deeper our relationship gets with Him, we are to protect our reverence for Him. If Judas Iscariot and Ananias and Sapphira and King Herod Agrippa were not delt with as quickly as they were, the risk to corrupt and negatively influence God's people would have been ungraciously great, His true children who fear Him would be easily led astray into darkness … into a lifestyle of idolatry all over again which could eventually lead many more to committing the Unforgivable Sin. Therefore, to ensure saving many … a few were sacrificed to be made an example of what not to do, that not even repentance could deliver them from eternal death in Hades fire (ref. Hebrews chapter 6). The more we know Jesus, the closer we can be to forfeit the entrusted holiness of His divine grace and mercy that flows in and through His chosen servants. Because of this, He demonstrated His gracious rath to help protect our hearts from becoming conceited, arrogant, prideful, and lusting over money. In this way, the effectiveness of the church will better remain knowing the consequences of an unpardonable act through the God-fearing. Jesus, full of mercy and grace, quickened His rath to protect and preserve His church and bride – those small and great among it.

# RECENT EVENTS

God spoke to me in 2016 right before the presidential election and said: "Son you will watch during the next administration's reign how Satan will use politics as an end-time strategy to divide my church." Not just me but we Americans and many throughout the world saw during President Trump's 4-year termed presidency where the demonic forces were in full-effect to bring much division in the church – The Body of Christ, as observed in the United States. This is coined also by the changing of the US's guiding principles to keep "state and church separate" – we learned that during Trump's presidency that he haphazardly changed this rule of the land and permitted churches to preach politics and their influences to their congregations at the pulpit. This change caused confusion as he was not authorized to do so, but it permitted a false sense of security for a short while, and as such much church and political divisiveness ensued from 2016 to early 2021. You can go to: https://www.peoplesworld. org/article/the-terrible-10-church-state-separation-lowlights-of-d onald-trumps-presidency/ and read up on this article in more detail on Trump's attempt to abolish this guiding principal. Since then, preachers are unrelentingly preaching politics behind the pulpits (even to this very day) … to the extent of having used scare tactics to influence congregations to vote again for Trump in the 2020 elections if they wanted the favor of God to rest on the United States of America. In one case, furthered this white-evangelical movement with an ultimatum … if you do not vote in this manner, God is sending a great judgement on this country. Another well-known evangelist minister who is having seemingly great tent meetings in California had the audacity to say on his ministerial social media platform: "that you cannot be a true Christian if you vote democrat." For this section I prefer to leave names of these ministers out. I believe many of these ministers are skating on lukewarm ice and are dangerously close to engaging into the blaspheming against The Holy Spirit territory – I pray they repent and turn back to their first love. In Jesus name I pray, amen.

Although many US ministers, predominately white evangelicals, have falsely prophesied Trump's reelection directly or supported those who did and came into spiritual agreement with them, God spoke to me differently in parable form on September 12, 2020 as outlined on our ministry's Facebook page, *Living on the Rock Ministries*, as follows:

"There is a man who was born into wealth, was a so-called 'believer' since youth, thinks as though he has nothing to repent of, prides himself with himself - exalts himself, tears down those who disagree with him, extremely haughty, spews lies, divorces to remarry several times now, swings to varying political sides for self-gain, consistency is far from him, he delights in double-mindedness, downplays the impact of a current plague, perpetuates gossip unending … daily! Has so-called ministers pray over him, in the sight of all Americans … Looks on the outside as though it's good … But internally he thinks, 'I got you'! Many so-called 'believers' are impressed with his outward appearance … Most believers in fact … All the while blinded by Satan of his deathly fruit - namely scare tactics. He's seemingly the people's choice like the evil one, King Saul - yes, who later blasphemed against The Holy Spirit in the scriptures - who then was consigned to eternal death. He can be reelected, but this would keep him enthralled of self, limiting true justice for all. Sadly, only a small remnant truly sees through his evil deception! Do you see it"? This was the parable God spoke into my spirit with great clarity and urgency on that day (9/12/20).

Why do I mention these things, and how does it have anything to do with the teaching and counseling of the Unforgivable Sin?

Answer: to help authenticate this book that the Lord called me to write for His glory. This is not aimed to insight nonsensical quarrels, but rather irrefutably honor God, His son Jesus and The Holy Spirit with the hope and trust many will allow the Spirit of the Lord to teach on this subject, Unforgivable Sin, Biblically. And the source God chose to bring clarity through His vessel, me, to demonstrate His stamp of spiritual approval – He used the product of Special Education, one who had a learning disability all throughout elementary school to now teach on one of the most controversial subjects of the Bible. Glory to God Almighty and blessed be He forever and ever!

I believe in these next two examples of specific individuals who perished during their popular ministries flourishing, they were given ample grace and mercy to repent during their church-idolatry - being lukewarm in the active presence of the Lord. I further trust it came to the point of no return, and God's rath graciously and long-sufferingly was finally invoked. Here, and with God's approval, I will share the names of those who broke faith and forfeited God's holiness and therefore blasphemed against The Holy Spirit in recent times passed. This synoptic and spiritual view is not aimed to encapsulate all peoples who committed this act in recent times past here in the US, no not at all – just those examples where popularity and fame and the love of money were central in these examples and to help bring clarity to this teaching for this subject, Unforgivable Sin. Furthermore, this is not to shame the fans, families and friends of those in the following examples. No, not at all! It is heartbreaking the myriad of followers these examples and their ministries who felt deeply hurt by their deaths – I sympathize with them in this reality. As a shepherd, called and chosen by God the Father, it is no shepherds' desire that anyone would perish in their sins – this character comes from God. Please understand this. Please!

I will lead us into scripture to preface the following examples. As it is written: "The elders who direct the affairs of the church well are worthy of double honor, especially those whose work is preaching and teaching. For Scripture says, 'Do not muzzle an ox while it is treading out the grain,' and 'The worker deserves his wages.' Do not entertain an accusation against an elder unless it is brought by two or three witnesses. But those elders who are sinning you are to reprove before everyone, so that the others may take warning. I charge you, in the sight of God and Christ Jesus and the elect angels, to keep these instructions without partiality, and to do nothing out of favoritism" (1 Timothy 5:17–21). This scripture speaks for itself, and if the following examples would have listened to the voice of the Lord, The Holy Spirit, like King David with the prophet Nathan, these brothers would still be alive today and honoring the Lord and serving Him with all humility and gratitude – I truly believe this. For this teaching however, it is essential we look into these elder's (teachers, apologists and prophets) lifestyle to glean into their lukewarm and blaspheme against The Holy Spirit sins.

In this first example, we will evaluate the false prophet, Kim Clement. This is said based on his latter years, as his former years may have been at one time fruitful in holy manner. Thus, as it is also written: "Therefore, son of man, say to your people, 'If someone who is righteous disobeys, that person's former righteousness will count for nothing. And if someone who is wicked repents, that person's former wickedness will not bring condemnation. The righteous person who sins will not be allowed to live even though they were formerly righteous'" (Ezekiel 33:12). It is in this biblical context we will evaluate the false prophet, Kim Clement.

The following can be verified against Kim Clement's YouTube video titled, *Trump 2020 Prophecy – Kim Clement*, published December 19, 2020 but dated in the video's caption as February 22, 2014 (roughly two years prior to his death in 2016). In this video Kim prophesied about the next in-coming president, which became Donald Trump, regarding his wise and noble character and his fierce opposition, which are as follows in Kim Clement's own words:

- Kim Clement said to the effect: "He would be a man of prayer";
  - This is false as Trump never showed evidence that he prayed but many prayed for him publicly, nor did he feel as though he needed to repent about anything as he so mentioned in an interview, that he does no wrong so he doesn't have to repent – repentance is a reverent act of prayer. According to the word of God, we are all filthy as dirty rags and have sinned and fallen short to God's glory;
- Kim Clement said to the effect: "He would have choice words, one who does not speak too much, people would say about him that he does not speak enough";
  - This is false since much of Trump's words on social media, namely Twitter, he spoke much divisiveness and nonsensical controversies unrelentingly – to the point he was banned on social media since early 2021 when he incited the Capital's insurrection with his loyal and primarily white-supremacist followers to intimidate to the point of influencing the reversal attempt of the election's result of Joe Biden as president-elect – which failed as Joe Biden became the 46th president of the United States of America; and
- Kim Clement said to the effect: "Of this man many would say impeach, impeach, but it shall be nay, nay says the Lord";
  - This was false because Trump was legally and justly impeached twice, making it in the court vernacular, "yay – yay" not 'nay-nay' as he prophesied.

Kim Clement died a false prophet – no record of him publicly repenting prior to his death. Thus, he died the same year Trump was inaugurated in 2016 – same year God spoke to me about the end-time evil strategy of politics.

Other concerning facts regarding Kim Clement. However, I don't treat this matter as concrete as the YouTube video where you can witness Kim's words from his own mouth. Nonetheless, an online article would also suggest that since 2006 Kim had been prophesying specific time limits for the miracles to come to pass and it never did, for example ... the rapper Eminem would be a voice for Christianity and conversion would be on his house he said, and in the same year that Stephen King would make movies that glorify God. Per Kim, these events were to come to pass within the year 2006. I paraphrased here, but it is all substantiated in an article online titled, *Kim Clement: In 2006, God says, 'I will now multiply the anointing on the ages from 8 to 17. They shall become the voices to this Nation'*. No substantial evidence of these prophecies having come to pass within the time limits in his "thus says the Lord" prophecies – none that I was able to locate online.

Fame, popularity, and money became a church-idolatry that led to Kim Clement's spiritual demise – it is not my place to say where Kim's soul is, but it is between God and him. My concern, Jesus taught His disciples that the closer you draw to Him and as His Holy Spirit flows through you for His glory, be careful not to love money. As the love of money is the root of much sin and evil, and He also said that it is easier for a camel to go through the eye of a needle than a rich man or woman to enter the Kingdom of Heaven. Jesus further coined in the Gospels that you cannot serve two masters (darkness and truth) simultaneously, you either serve one or the other – this is ultimately where God's children end up – serving one or the other (Satan/money or God/truth). I believe there was a former time Kim Clement once was activated and entrusted with The Holy Spirit, but denied his faith somewhere along the line of fame, popularity and monetary riches – leading to insulting the Spirit of the Lord by prophesying out of his flesh presumptuously, and in his own understanding, rather than by the Spirit of the Lord – eventually causing his Unforgivable Sin. How? By continuously prophesying with "thus says the Lord" prophecies with specific time limits and them not coming to pass. There is no prophet of the Lord that ever got it right some of the times, and not 100% of the time. For example, Enoch the son of Jared never falsely prophesied; Moses never falsely prophesied; Elijah never falsely prophesied; Jeremiah never falsely prophesied; Ezekiel never falsely prophesied; Malachi never falsely prophesied; Jesus our Lord never falsely prophesied; apostle Peter never falsely prophesied. A false prophet is defined in the Bible quite simply as follows: "If what a prophet proclaims in the name of the LORD does not take place or come true, that is a message the LORD has not spoken. That prophet has spoken presumptuously, so do not be alarmed" (Deuteronomy 18:22). However, there were many false prophets in the Old Testament and we were warned in the New Testament that many false prophets will arise in the end-time – this we see irrefutably in our generation and can expect it in the next and until Jesus' second coming. Since God is the one and only avenger, we leave the soul of our brother Kim Clement in the hands of our Almighty God, lest we place our judgmental thoughts as if we are a god – the verdict of the soul is solely for the Lord's discretion and judgement! Not that it is of any significant importance, but it is believed Kim Clement died of a brain bleed and cancer of some sort. To this effect I am reminded of the following scripture: "Furthermore, just as they did not think it worthwhile to retain the knowledge of God, so God gave them over to a depraved mind, so that they do what ought not to be done" (Romans 1:28). From here, relative to Kim Clement's fallacious Kingdom service as false prophet, I believe he broke faith and forfeited God's holiness, thus committing blaspheme against The Holy Spirit.

What defense is there when preaching the Gospels yet living a life contrary to what is preached? The Bible calls this hypocrisy. Jesus spoke about this and said: " ...they have received their reward in full" (Matthew 6:2). In this second example, this was the life Ravi Zacharias lived, while the world looked at him, especially in the Christian circles worldwide, as a highly renowned apologist and author of roughly 30 books. Thus, an apologist is a theological term that characterizes "apologist" as a defender of the Gospels. What defense to the love of Christ is this, relative to Ravi Zacharias' lifestyle when for years leading up to his death in May 2020 was living an adulterous lifestyle as a married man? I ask on the premise of the following scripture: "Jesus replied, 'Anyone who loves me will obey my teaching. My Father will love them, and we will come to them and make our home with them. Anyone who does not love me will not obey my teaching. These words you hear are not my own; they belong to the Father who sent me'" (John 14:22-24). In like manner of Kim Clement, there is no record of Ravi Zacharias ever publicly repenting – both Kim and Ravi were deserving of public repentance, but no record of it. Not that it is of any significant importance, but it is believed Ravi Zacharias died of spinal cancer. To this effect the following scripture comes to mind: "If anyone causes one of these little ones—those who believe in me—to stumble, it would be better for them to have a large millstone hung around their neck and to be drowned in the depths of the sea" (Matthew 18:6). I am not led to spend much time on Ravi Zacharias' accusations, but they are exhaustively available online. One might be thinking, in this particular matter, how does the prior scripture line up? Answer: the word of God in many instances teaches us to help others turn from their unrighteousness (ref. Psalm 51:13 and I Peter 4:8 as examples), so when a person like Ravi Zacharias professes to be a servant of the Most High God as an apologist and turns women-Christians into his perverted desires of fornication he is doing the opposite of Jesus' teachings; thus, causing them to stumble. Like I said, I do not feel spiritually compelled to go over Ravi Zacharias' hypocritical accounts but invite you to certainly substantiate what it is I write on with your own online research study.

Similarly to Kim Clement the false prophet, Ravi Zacharias died a false teacher and apologist through the tainting of his fallacious Kingdom service as hypocrite. How do I know this? I know by this … as it is written: " If you really keep the royal law found in Scripture, "Love your neighbor as yourself," you are doing right. But if you show favoritism, you sin and are convicted by the law as lawbreakers. For whoever keeps the whole law and yet stumbles at just one point is guilty of breaking all of it. For he who said, "You shall not commit adultery," also said, "You shall not murder." If you do not commit adultery but do commit murder, you have become a lawbreaker" (James 2:8-11). This also holds true in Ravi Zacharias' case that even though we know not of any murder he committed (although potentially he did in his heart at some point), he did commit adulty continually and sinned against the Law of God continually, making him a lawbreaker – guilty of all the law especially as his sins caused others to sin – compounding sins against God. I believe Ravi Zacharias had ample time to repent over his 74 years of life, 40 of which in Christian ministry, to our forgiving God but also to his spiritual demise coming by the unrepented hidden lifestyle of church-idolatry it came to a place of no return to good standing with God. The Book of Hebrews explains this matter as follows: " It is impossible for those who have once been enlightened, who have tasted the heavenly gift, who have shared in the Holy Spirit, who have tasted the goodness of the word of God and the powers of the coming age and who have fallen away, to be brought back to repentance. To their loss they are crucifying the Son of God all over again and subjecting him to public disgrace" (Hebrews 6:4-6). This is a perfect example in Ravi Zacharias' testimony that speaks to the lukewarm condition of a leader of one of God's lighthouses (the church), where Jesus warned the leader of the church that He was about to spit him (the leader of the church) out of His mouth (ref. Revelation 3:16). This means, that although you still have a chance to repent, if you don't repent of your lukewarm condition it would eventually equal to Jesus' total rejection – Ravi Zacharias experienced Jesus' total rejection – quite similarly to Kim Clement, but the difference as I understand it is this ... Kim Clement blasphemed against The Holy Spirit by doing wrong with the prophetic gift to the point of breaking faith and forfeiting God's holiness; whereas, Ravi Zacharias repeatedly committed lukewarm acts (repeated church leadership idolatry in the area of adultery) to the point, figuratively, Jesus spit him out of His mouth – spiritually and physically removing his light stand (church). I am convinced, repeated unrepenting lukewarm sinful acts leads to Blaspheme Against The Holy Spirit. Unrepenting lukewarm (church leadership idolatry) sin acts fails to uphold faithfulness to God and His holiness.

I trust that these aforementioned testimonies of false ministers,

not that it is in entirety of falsehood in recent past, no not at all –
for there are many right now perpetuating falsehood – but this has
lent a teaching hand and through exposure and analyzing the
wrongdoings Biblically that we understand in greater detail the seed
of blaspheme against The Holy Spirit, which is being lukewarm and
the Unforgivable Sin itself, which is blaspheme against The Holy
Spirit. Lukewarm is a church leader who is actively committing
unrepenting church idolatry. And blaspheme against The Holy Spirit
is a God-fearing person who: 1) breaks faith with God; and 2)
forfeits God's holiness. I like how Dr. Howard-John Wesley taught
on stealing God's glory, which is a character of blaspheme against
The Holy Spirit, on his YouTube video published 7/19/2021 titled,
*"Crime and Punishment"* as he mentioned: "spiritual plagiarism."
This was coined when Moses at the rock of Meribah the second
time broke faith and forfeited God's holiness, where Moses made
the miracle look as though he and his brother Aaron performed
it … the miracle was God providing water for the Israelites through
the rock, to quench the needed thirst of God's children, again, for
a second time. This story found in the Book of Numbers chapter
20 versus 6-12 was paramount to the teachings on the Unforgivable
Sin in this book. Good to witness sound preaching and teaching
on this matter as Dr. Howard-John Wesley preached as mentioned
in his YouTube video: *"Crime and Punishment"*. This is a video I
recommend watching to help instill the Holy Fear of the Lord to
always give God all the praise and glory, especially as He performs
miracles in your life or through you as a ministerial vessel – He and
only He deserves it all.

# SATAN'S ROLE

What is Satan's role? As the prince of the air as referred to in The Book of Ephesian's 2:2, his mission is to steal, kill and destroy as also referred to in The Book of John 10:10. Jesus refers to Satan in The Book of John 8:44 as follows: "You belong to your father, the devil, and you want to carry out your father's desires. He was a murderer from the beginning, not holding to the truth, for there is no truth in him. When he lies, he speaks his native language, for he is a liar and the father of lies." Thus, Satan over the thousands of years has been deceiving and tricking many by using the Holy Scriptures in a perverted way to cause them to stumble. It was Satan in the garden who cunningly tricked Eve, seduced her in essence, by convincing her to disobey God's command, which was to refrain from eating from the tree of knowledge (ref. Genesis 2:17). Satan twisted God's words to trick Eve; thus, influenced Eve to disobey God's command and she caused Adam to do the same. The root cause of this disobedience to God's command was the enemy (Satan) used trickery to pervert the truth of God's word and influenced Eve to rebel and inadvertently caused her husband to as well. This caused a death, also known as a spiritual separation, between Adam and Eve together and their relationship with God. The wages of sin (disobedience to God's word) is death – in other words, the returned consequence of sin is death. This is not a physical death, but a spiritual death – a relationship that has been severed between Adam and Eve as one flesh and God. As Satan rebelled in Heaven, his aim is to cause rebellion on the earth to separate God's children and their relationship with Him. We see in the prior passage of scripture where Jesus was keenly emphasizing how Satan is the source of lies; thus, as his 'native' tongue – he is the king liar and deceiver. This means, his role is to take the truth, manipulate it, replace it with lies and try to get as many to follow his evil in the process.

To paraphrase, as referred to in The Book of Revelation 12:2, Satan knows his time is short on this earth … therefore, his strategy is to deceive and lead as many people as possible to Hades, even God's elect if he can. God's elect can be understood as pastors, prophets, apostles, teachers, evangelists – those called to preach and teach God's word. These are considered His elect. On this matter, Unforgivable Sin, Satan wants people to think they have committed this sin when they never came close to it … especially those who don't know the Bible … but unfortunately, those who do know the Bible, most of them today teach this matter incorrectly … false teaching is in motion that Satan takes malicious joy in. Additionally, some teachers of the Gospels avoid the topic altogether. Consequently, the scriptures warn us: "my people are destroyed from lack of knowledge. 'Because you have rejected knowledge, I also reject you as my priests; because you have ignored the law of your God, I also will ignore your children'" (Hosea 4:6). Following, I will provide four tested-faith experience testimonies that will bring light to how Satan deceives people: first, where Satan deceived a brother in a men's recovery home sanctuary, where there were other brothers receiving the teaching on the Unforgivable Sin when a false grace conviction befell; second, where Satan deceived a co-worker regarding his choice to marry a non-believer; third, where the absence of knowledge had the potential to improperly teach through the ignorant minister and evangelist friend of mine; and fourth, where Satan used a 30-year Sunday school teacher to distort the truth and created his own doctrine to explain his false knowledge of this matter. These testimonial accounts will be in chronological order.

# FALSE GRACE CONVICTION (MEN'S HOME)

"Why should I serve God if I have committed this Unforgiveable Sin?" This was a false grace response I received during a time I was preaching at a men's recovery home. I had brushed up on the matter of the Unforgivable Sin, and one of the brothers in the group raised his hand while seemingly stricken with immense fear in his eyes and said what he said. He further went on and mentioned he was once a part of an Aztecan pagan religion and was in terror thinking he had committed the Unforgivable Sin because of their past ungodly worship. As a new convert of the Christian faith, certainly my brother was falsely convicted, and was swiftly vindicated by the Spirit of Truth as God would have me to minister to him and the rest of the group – that being a product of your environment and ignorant of the truth cannot cause you to sin in this way. Ignorance is incapable of committing the Unforgivable Sin. As a quick reminder … the Unforgivable Sin is referred to in the New Testament as blasphemy against The Holy Spirit. So certainly, as God lives eternally, my brother didn't come close to committing this sin. Apostle Paul affirms it Biblically in his testimony as follows: "Even though I was once a blasphemer and a persecutor and a violent man, I was shown mercy because I acted in ignorance and unbelief." (1 Timothy 1:13).

Yet, if Satan could have kept the brother thinking what he was falsely thinking, then certainly he could have happily led him astray. The Devil is a liar!

# MARITAL DECISION (CO-WORKER)

My friend, Wade, a previous co-worker of mine was deeply deceived by the wicked one. I have asked Wade to share some of his testimony on this deception in this book to help spiritually substantiate my tested-faith experience on the matter, Unforgivable Sin, but I summarize some of that here to coin the reality of Satin's deceiving power on this subject.

Wade had mentioned to me that he felt he had committed the Unforgivable Sin because of his choice to marry his unbelieving wife. At the time he had been taking psychological medications and seeing multiple psychologists regarding his anxiety, and for another symptom he called "zaps" – where it felt like his brain was being shocked, and the shockwaves would flow to his limbs. I asked him if I could pray for him, and he immediately said yes. So, right there in our office we held each other's hands, and I began to pray, and immediately the Spirit of the Lord and His glory was heavily upon us – a divine manifested prayer came through my lips, prophesying the healing of Wade's mind. Once the glory of God ran its full course in prayer, relief was immediately felt – Wade mentioned he felt heat throughout his body during the prayer. After that prayer, Wade never went back to taking the psychological prescriptions, nor seen another psychologist since. All glory to God Almighty, blessed be He forever and ever for the psychological healing miracle He performed in Wade!

I had also comforted Wade about his choice in marriage, and that although he sinned by placing his wife above God – committing adultery … it is forgivable. I also shared with him the scriptures Apostle Paul wrote to counsel the churches in Corinth, where in 1 Corinthians 7:12–14 says: "To the rest I say this (I, not the Lord): If any brother has a wife who is not a believer and she is willing to live with him, he must not divorce her. And if a woman has a husband who is not a believer and he is willing to live with her, she must not divorce him. For the unbelieving husband has been sanctified through his wife, and the unbelieving wife has been sanctified through her believing husband. Otherwise, your children would be unclean, but as it is, they are holy." Clearly, my friend Wade has been spiritually vindicated and set free, and now more hopeful than ever to believe his wife, too, will be saved by the blood of Jesus.

# LACK OF KNOWLEDGE
# (MINISTER & EVANGELIST)

During a casual discussion after dinner with a dear friend, years back, who was and still is a minister and evangelist, who has been serving God in the ministry for decades, once told me: "The Unforgivable Sin is not in the Bible, it is a man-made doctrine." Mind you, it is clearly stated as mentioned earlier in this book in 3 out of the 4 Gospels (Matthew, Mark, and Luke). This was scary, because my friend who ministers to others has the potential to wrongly teach others on this matter. I'll never forget, at the table after dinner how shocked I was. The conversation came up about the topic, and when discussing it, hearing this was so alarming ... I remember my Spirit was so grieved ... stirred ... deeply provoked! I took a deep breath, prayed in my conscience asking God for guidance ... thinking, how am I as an immature Christian going to correct a mature one – a minister far longer in the ministry than I? This was my thought. God quickened my Spirit to ask my friend: "Can I show you in the Bible"? I immediately discerned the resistance from his countenance – his body language refused before he uttered a word – pride swelled in his heart – humility was far from him. He would then angrily say: "No you do not need to show me." Then the Spirit of the Lord said into my Spirit, "Drop it"! At this, I realized the seed of truth was planted according to the will of The Father, and to pray (water) over the seed of life (truth) in my secret place believing by faith God would germinate His truth in my friend and grow roots (knowledge) in his heart. Although I do not know for certain at this time I write, whether my friend has allowed God to correct him to bring forth the Biblical knowledge he then lacked, but I hope and trust He has corrected my friend. Further, it is my prayer my friend received the knowledge and is producing fruit out of his obedience to the truth. Obedience? Yes, just because we have the knowledge doesn't mean we apply it ... Jesus said to His disciples, "You'll know them by their fruit" – this is to say that by a man or woman's actions, deeds, and speech you'll know their character. So, I say that to say this, if my friend teaches on this or counsels on it, rather than saying it is not in the Bible, I pray he speaks on it from the Bible … and if he doesn't fully understand it, I trust he'll refrain from teaching or counseling on it and give it to God until he matures in the knowledge on the matter, as God helps him understand.

## FALSE TEACHING (SUNDAY SCHOOL TEACHER)

This last example concerns me more than the one prior, where a 30-year Sunday school teacher and pastor at a nearby church, whom at the time I'd adored, knowing the words of Jesus on the Unforgivable Sin would say after dinner years back: "The only Unforgivable Sin is unrepented sin". By this time, I was already called by God to write this book, so you might imagine how stirred my Spirit was! In this case, unlike the prior one, God unleashed the gift of counsel with swiftness in me – sternly and authoritatively in Spirit correcting our friend pastor and Sunday school teacher on the matter – lovingly. Seemingly in a state of paralysis, our friend remained silent, but days after would start an array of text messages … trying to refute the knowledge. After several counters while praying each time, I reprimanded him in Jesus name as his false doctrine was dangerous, as it was leaning on his flawed understanding and because he didn't understand this matter in truth confidently, he attempted to refute it opinionatedly. That is dangerous! This goes against the teaching of God and His word, as His word in The Book of Revelation warns us not to add or subtract from His Holy Scriptures. Unfortunately, this is a matter I had to leave in God's hands, after exhausting every Holy Spirit guided avenue to correct this Sunday school teacher and lovingly win his heart over for God's glory. False teaching knowing the words of Jesus is much worse than lacking knowledge and not teaching on it and tarrying The Holy Spirit for the knowledge. The latter is spiritually wise. Jesus mentions to the effect: "Woe unto those who cause my weak to stumble" - the consequence He explains after this passage in the Bible is brutal (ref. Matthew 18:6)! As a called and chosen shepherd, there is nothing more stirring in my heart knowing someone is teaching falsely to others, especially a man or woman of God of the cloth (a minister), and in this case adding a false doctrine to God's eternally fixed and secure doctrine. That said, God has divorced our fellowship together since then.

Unfortunately, this apostate behavior is to be expected in these End Times – regarding false teaching. It is fitting to recite scripture spoken through the Apostle Paul as follows: "For the time will come when people will not put up with sound doctrine. Instead, to suit their own desires, they will gather around them a great number of teachers to say what their itching ears want to hear. They will turn their ears away from the truth and turn aside to myths" (2 Timothy 4:3-4). Again, very dangerous to behave as a minister in this way – having the potential to cause innocent people of weaker faith to be deceived and deprived/hindered of receiving true scriptural knowledge. Additionally, this falsehood has the potential for others to question themselves causing themselves inadvertent confusion. In either case, Satan would love to wreak havoc in the minds of those being deceived and falsely taught to steel the truth they could obtain through the Spirit of Truth.

# BREAKING THE
# DEVIL'S CURSE

One of the core missions of the Devil is to steal – this includes stealing the knowledge and understanding of God's children – you and me – all of us! Jesus coined this very evil mission best when He was teaching His disciples about the seed's parable: "Listen then to what the parable of the sower means: When anyone hears the message about the kingdom and does not understand it, the evil one comes and snatches away what was sown in their heart. This is the seed sown along the path" (Matthew 13:18-19). In this parable, Jesus was explaining different scenarios in which the seeds being sown are received ... the seed represents God's scriptures, holy and true. The enemy, the Devil, also known as Satan, does not want God's children to know and understand the Word of God, as people are powerless against the Devil's schemes without the knowledge and understanding of it. For example, just before Jesus started his ministry, He was tested in the desert during a 40-day fast ... where the Devil tempted Jesus first with bread as he knew Jesus was physically hungry as He had been fasting, but then the Devil continued to tempt Jesus as He combatted the Devil using the holy seeds (God's Word) to dismantle the Devil's schemes, which namely were and still are temptation and deception. If the Devil can tempt people and deceive us, we then become vulnerable and easy prey for his mission to lure us away from the protective truths of God's Eternal Word. Jesus is the perfect example of how to combat evil schemes directed by the Devil using the Word of God, and using the promising Word to "resist the devil and he will flee" as mentioned in James 4:7. It is time to break the Devil's curse of stealing peoples knowledge and set the captives free in Jesus name, amen, and secure and protect the Word of God in our hearts! Hallelujah! My friends … this is GOOD NEWS!

Following will detail some of the main factors God has keenly made me aware of regarding the evolution of man from early scripture days in the Old Testament, through New Testament, and into today's time. This will shed light on how trustworthy teaching gradually degraded over time, providing a deeper understanding to the reasoning, which will then help to solidify the teachings of this book and help others to better make sound judgement on trustworthy reading material. Thus, regarding the Word of God which is most trustworthy, to learn to read and interpret in Spirit and in Truth rather than by human understanding, which can fail us – I say it like this: good theology, though literal, only edifies the spiritual truth of God; bad theology of others does not compromise the spiritual truth of God when you learn to read in the Spirit – so in either case you will know the difference. This is to say, the human study of God's word doesn't need to be the basis of your understanding of it when you allow the Holy Spirit to be your teacher and interpreter.

The Unforgivable Sin has been a Biblical topic that over the many years passed since Moses' time, the accurate knowledge of it has been severely compromised – this is the curse of the enemy. Therefore, our true knowledge is rooted in the uncompromised Word of God and His Holy Spirit in conjunction. Why do I say this? Well, today more often than not, any teaching or preaching of this topic is severely distorted, or as mentioned earlier in the book, avoided altogether. The most common falsehood of this teaching is that this Unforgivable Sin can only be committed by a non-believer of Jesus Christ. This is a lie straight from the pit of Hades! Let me be clear, I am not addressing the falsehood being manifested through flesh (human beings), but the evil spirits behind the flesh. Thus, most teachers of the Word of God who deal with this topic, believe in their hearts that what they are teaching is true and accurate, yet they're deceived by the enemy.

Let's go further ... deeper ... getting a glimpse back in the Old Testament of the seed of deception on Unforgivable Sin. First written and Biblically documented, Unforgivable Sin, was in Moses' testimony at the Rock of Meribah the second time. When this sin was committed, God did not quickly correct the issue, as Moses was still used physically by God for a while to get the Israelites close to the promised land. In Spirit, God showed me how this lapse in time for correction caused many to believe that Moses performed the miracle at the Rock, and since then this misperception continues to this day – where in some religious circles Moses is regarded even more greatly than our Lord and Savior, Jesus Christ, who represented the Rock at Meribah. This has caused much deception then, and increased deception now ever since the event. The evil spirit behind the deception was our advisory at work for darkness – since then it has caused various religions to be in spiritual conflict – even to the extreme of provoking wars. No need to detail these religions, lest we add nonsensical controversies that does not bring God honor. I am hopeful this book with Holy Spirit's help, bring many into the truth of God on this matter and renew their hope and gain freedom.

To close here, the question is: how do we break the curse of the enemy on the Unforgivable Sin? We need the spiritual knowledge of the Word of God in our hearts with uncompromising assurance given by Holy Spirit, our teacher and reminder. I leave you with this incredibly important scripture to keep us reminded, maintaining proper perspective as we carry on in life: "It is impossible for those who have once been enlightened, who have tasted the heavenly gift, who have shared in the Holy Spirit, who have tasted the goodness of the word of God and the powers of the coming age and who have fallen away, to be brought back to repentance. To their loss they are crucifying the Son of God all over again and subjecting him to public disgrace" (Hebrews 6:4 – 6). This is truth, contrary to the deception of the enemy leading many to believe they have committed the Unforgivable Sin or forfeited their souls ... the truth of the matter is all sins but Blaspheme Against The Holy Spirit as the only exception are forgivable through repentance. Ignorance of the truth comes nowhere close to the Unforgivable Sin, as it is written: "I thank Christ Jesus our Lord, who has given me strength, that he considered me trustworthy, appointing me to his service. Even though I was once a blasphemer and a persecutor and a violent man, I was shown mercy because I acted in ignorance and unbelief. The grace of our Lord was poured out on me abundantly, along with the faith and love that are in Christ Jesus" (1 Timothy 1:12 – 14). The truth sets us free - amen, amen and amen! Thank You Jesus!!!

# FINAL EXHORTATION –
# AN ENTERTAINMENT PIECE

In the middle of writing this book, God burdened my heart for the souls in the entertainment business. Let me be clear though … I am not talking about those who have the evidence of the Living Christ in their behavior, like Denzel Washington. Clearly this brother has been touched by God … his testimony says so … what he does today in the industry and in society was prophesied over his life by an old black woman in church when Denzel was just a little boy … God has been faithful to Denzel. A man who worked feverishly to get small acts in the 80's, to now an explosive acting powerhouse and role model, yet under the fear of the Lord. I am not speaking about a burden for the Denzels' … no, not at all!

Rather, my heart was burdened when I heard one of the members from a rap group, Island Boys, talking on Twitter saying: "I gave my soul to the devil". This burdened my heart! A young man, FlyySoulja, talking about his experience of giving his soul to the devil among his followers on Twitter in November of 2021. He mentioned that his motive was to get famous and rich, and to do so he had to make a sacrifice … his sacrifice was his soul, rather than a person he loves. THE DEVIL IS A LIAR! He also mentioned that he was not feeling good ever since he chose to do what he did, and that his anxiety was high. To a seasoned believer in Christ, this feeling is of no surprise, as God our Creator and First Love gave us a portion of faith free-of-charge. Judging by his Twitter video, he may have been around 20 years of age, my guess. Regardless, he is a very young man who has his whole life ahead to look forward to, but so influenced by fame and money – a very common theme for so many in all age groups. Obviously, knowing the scriptures it warns us not to love money, and that money is the root of all evil, or depending on the translation, the root of all kinds of evil. That said, if Jesus in red letters teaches us not to love money, then there is a critical reason why.

Here, FlyySoulja, a young man certainly unaware of the love of Christ, whom is his, whether knowingly or unknowingly, First Love. The First Love, Jesus Christ, has all power and authority over all realms of the Heavenlies. Jesus has dominion over death and life – Hades and Heaven. Certainly, FlyySoulja is operating out of a spirit of naivete – he has been deceived to love money and fame more than Creator – his First Love – his willing Redeemer – his willing Savior. FlyySoulja is redeemable – not because I say so, but our Living Christ. Let me help explain …

Imagine a so-called man of God who was widely known for killing and imprisoning Christians. Granted, this was during a time the Gospel of Jesus was just being preached by his first disciples, but nonetheless, a God-fearing man killing the followers of God's only begotten Son. Strange, right!?! How can you believe in God and yet kill the followers of His Son? As extremely weird this dichotomy may seem, this is the true testimony of a man named Saul – of course this is only a fragment of his testimony before being converted himself and later becoming a powerhouse Christ-follower. FlyySoulja didn't come anywhere close to Saul's egregious acts of murder and imprisoner of Christians. Learning from this book there is only one sin that is unforgivable – and it does not include the love of money and fame. Jesus even gives the church leadership a charge in The Book of Revelation to repent of their love of money. FlyySoulja is not even at this level of concern, since he is clearly naive to the love of Christ that is far richer than money and fame – Jesus is willing to forgive this double idolatry. If murder and imprisoning innocent people was forgiven for Saul – then the love of money and fame is forgivable for our brother FlyySoulja. Even though he said these empty words: "I gave my soul to the Devil" – these were words that do not fulfill a purpose for God's plan, and FlyySoulja and all of us who have spoken empty words, unfulfilling for God's Kingdom, we will all hold an account to those words spoken from our lips; however, we have the assurance of Life Eternal through our repentance. As the scriptures also describe there are unintentional sins and intentional sins, both of which are forgivable. Saul knew that his Old Testament God said: "Thou shall not murder". Yet, Saul thought he was justified because he himself was ignorant of the spiritual realization that the Messiah prophesied in Old Testament had come to proclaim the good news and set captives free, among many other good acts of kindness. Out of his spiritual ignorance and spiritual blindness, he was forgiven.

Get this ... Saul would become Paul The Apostle of Christ Jesus, who ends up writing over two thirds of the New Testament Scriptures. Wow! Here is what Paul writes - under the anointing of Holy Spirit about ignorance and unbelief (or spiritual blindness):

"I thank Christ Jesus our Lord, who has given me strength, that he considered me trustworthy, appointing me to his service. Even though I was once a blasphemer and a persecutor and a violent man, I was shown mercy because I acted in ignorance and unbelief. The grace of our Lord was poured out on me abundantly, along with the faith and love that are in Christ Jesus. Here is a trustworthy saying that deserves full acceptance: Christ Jesus came into the world to save sinners—of whom I am the worst. But for that very reason I was shown mercy so that in me, the worst of sinners, Christ Jesus might display his immense patience as an example for those who would believe in him and receive eternal life. Now to the King eternal, immortal, invisible, the only God, be honor and glory for ever and ever. Amen" (1 Timothy 1:12-17).

So, to FlyySoulja and many others in the entertainment industry who are under the deception of a life-long binding contract with the Devil on the matter of your souls, brothers and sisters, God loves you and wants you to return back to Him! Repent of your double idolatry and be born again – He will be faithful to save you. That my friends is GOOD NEWS (The Gospel of Jesus Christ). Soak in these following words into your conscience for a great hope and trust of God's promise of Salvation over your lives, should you choose Him:

"For God so loved the world that he gave his one and only Son, that whoever believes in him shall not perish but have eternal life. For God did not send his Son into the world to condemn the world, but to save the world through him. Whoever believes in him is not condemned, but whoever does not believe stands condemned already because they have not believed in the name of God's one and only Son. This is the verdict: Light has come into the world, but people loved darkness instead of light because their deeds were evil. Everyone who does evil hates the light and will not come into the light for fear that their deeds will be exposed. But whoever lives by the truth comes into the light, so that it may be seen plainly that what they have done has been done in the sight of God" (John 3.16-21).

Therefore, and to the entertainment community – God is willing and able to forgive you. Remember, the Devil was cast out of Heaven as Lucifer, who before his name Satan came, he was first an angel for God in the Heavenlies – out of his arrogance, however, God cast him out of Heaven. Ever since then, the mission of the Devil and his demon-spirits is to kill, steel and destroy God's creation, mankind, as he and they know their time is short – and one day eternal fire will be their everlasting dwelling place (along with the Godless and wicked people of the earth). Don't let that be the place for your souls – REPENT! Closing on the following encouraging words of the Father in Heaven: "Say to them, As surely as I live, declares the Sovereign LORD, I take no pleasure in the death of the wicked, but rather that they turn from their ways and live. Turn! Turn from your evil ways! … '" (Ezekiel 33:11).

# SUMMATION

Do you have a good understanding of the Unforgivable Sin? If you made it this far in the book, you should be an expert on it and able to teach it. Right? Seriously, it is my hope that you have been blessed with a solid understanding of the teaching on the Unforgivable Sin – *The Blaspheme Against The Holy Spirit.*

Through the grace poured out by God, following will summarize the main constructs of the teachings of this Unforgivable Sin, starting with a flowchart to help coin the teaching with some visual reinforcement, especially for the visual learners' (like myself), then followed by a concise annotative synopsis to recap:

A recap of the Unforgivable Sin Progression, using Moses' testimony in a paraphrasing manner. So, Moses at the Rock of

Meribah the second time stole or otherwise plagiarized God's glory which was breaking faith with God (this was a lukewarm stage and would have been repent-able), but then to make matters worse, Moses disobeys God's command which was the forfeiting of God's holiness – all of which in the sight of thousands of Israelites and in the active presence of the Holy Spirit – this was his committing of the Unforgivable Sin. Let me break it down:

1. Moses broke faith with God by making the miracle God brought as if it were his own, when he said to the Israelites in the sight and active presence of the Holy Spirit: "must we do this for you." Moses made it sound as though the miracle came from him and his brother Aaron. This was a lukewarm phase and would have been repent-able. But ...

2. Moses then forfeits God's holiness when he disobeyed God's specific command to speak to the Rock (which was representative of Jesus Christ) and rather struck the Rock.

Thus, Aaron, as high priest, had a spiritual duty to God to correct Moses but didn't – making Aaron an accomplice to Moses' Unforgivable Sin of blaspheme against The Holy Spirit. The consequence of this was Aaron was commanded to die shortly after the committal of the Unforgivable Sin; Moses was commanded to die after leading the Israelites close to the Promised Land where he could see it from afar, and there on the top of Mount Nebo dies. Although Moses and his brother Aaron were once destined by the favor of God to live in the Promised Land flowing with milk and honey, they committed the Unforgivable Sin and were commanded by God to die.

To fully bridge understanding of the Unforgivable Sin, we had to journey into the waters of Old Testament to attain exact interpretation based on the heart of the Father in Heaven, blessed be He. This was in following and consistent with a theological guideline called: the law of first mention. In this manner, also guided by Holy Spirit, we used Moses' testimony where God first defined this sin where referred to by Jesus roughly fifteen hundred years later in the New Testament as blasphemy against The Holy Spirit. It was important not to just focus on the consequence referred to as unforgivable, but what made it unforgivable – the definitive explanation of the Unforgivable Sin. This will help to shatter the myriad of false teachings on the topic, which was also used by The Holy Spirit to inspire the teaching though this book – of course, with the help of scriptures and Him.

After gaining full understanding by the heart of the Father in Old Testament, we then ventured into the New Testament waters where Jesus would begin vital teachings to His disciples, which led them to fully reverence His Spirit, The Holy Spirit, when He was to go to be reunited with His Father, blessed be He, in heaven. This helped to seal the teaching with the Father's love, His agape love, so proper interpretation can begin to prevail on a more accelerated spiritual level, as the enemy had taken something that in Jesus' day (while flesh and blood) was just so well know and understood having been accurately passed down generationally prior to Jesus earthly ministry, to then be progressively diluted and distorted now centuries later.

Thus, Old and New Testaments bridged together in this teaching to gain the importance of getting realigned spiritually to accurately progress the true teaching hereafter – a spiritual calibration. This also aligns with the forward from Apostle Spear of Battle where he mentions to the effect that this sin has not been taught much over the last several hundred years. The time is ripe now and hereafter by the Spirit of God to bring proper understanding, a fullness to it, to dismantle the strategy of the enemy, Satan, to dwell in ignorance or confusion to do his evil bidding – to steel the hope and trust of many of God's children. The Devil is a liar!!! Time for generational blessings by the true teaching of this Unforgivable Sin, and no longer allow it to be a generational curse.

Now to close with a prophecy and loving exhortation … In Jesus Mighty Name, I prophesize that the teaching of this book will proliferate hope for those who feel as though their sins caused them such shame that their soul is unrecoverable even through repentance, and that many will obtain restored hope that they once had but confusion brought them to a place of hopelessness – the evidence of such hope will be realized by the Body of Christ no later than a year after the release of this book to public in a real evidential way that brings God The Father, His Son and His Holy Spirit all the Glory by His Great Name. Amen!

A loving exhortation to the leadership of the One Body of Christ, the bride of Christ, His invisible church – to you all I warn … Stop teaching falsely the Unforgivable Sin! If you must, avoid teaching this sin … even if you must tarry God until His Great Spirit – His Holy Spirit gives you supernatural and Scriptural understanding to do so. Do not teach based on your "opinions" – this is dangerously misleading and unholy! Sober up with this thought in the name of Jesus: As God-called and Holy Ghost-filled ministers, we are closer to the Unforgivable Sin than the flocks we Shepard and Steward – as the active presence of the Holy Spirit is in us. Stop teaching this fallacy on the matter of Unforgivable Sin: That this sin is committed by unbelievers who reject Jesus – this is the most widely spread false teaching on this matter – if you have been guilty in teaching this, REPENT like your life depends on it, as you have time to realign properly and to be Scripturally useful to the Body of Christ until He calls you home or until He comes again.

To all: believers, current unbelievers, rich, poor … do not hedge your luck on the unique outcome given Moses. Though he committed this sin first, blasphemed against The Holy Spirit, he was given divine opportunity to repent in the Spirit realm following his physical death. Do not take this chance! It could be everlastingly consequential! Now that you have the truth, as Jesus taught His disciples, which is now you and me in this life, avoid the committal of this Unforgivable Sin, and always reverence The Holy Spirit, and if you don't know Him, The Holy Spirit – learn to reverence Him with God's help. Therefore, this is how you should reverence The Holy Spirit as the Apostle Peter did, as it is written: "When the apostles in Jerusalem heard that Samaria had accepted the word of God, they sent Peter and John to Samaria. When they arrived, they prayed for the new believers there that they might receive the Holy

Spirit, because the Holy Spirit had not yet come on any of them; they had simply been baptized in the name of the Lord Jesus. Then Peter and John placed their hands on them, and they received the Holy Spirit. When Simon saw that the Spirit was given at the laying on of the apostles' hands, he offered them money and said, "Give me also this ability so that everyone on whom I lay my hands may receive the Holy Spirit." Peter answered: "May your money perish with you, because you thought you could buy the gift of God with money! You have no part or share in this ministry, because your heart is not right before God. Repent of this wickedness and pray to the Lord in the hope that he may forgive you for having such a thought in your heart. For I see that you are full of bitterness and captive to sin." Then Simon answered, "Pray to the Lord for me so that nothing you have said may happen to me" (Acts 8:14–24). Now, this was how Moses' brother, Aaron the High Priest, should have rebuked Moses before disobeying God's command at the Rock of Meribah the second time – with all reverence and conviction to The Holy Spirit, but did not. Peter had the swiftness and wisdom of The Holy Spirit through his reverence to aid in Simon's repentance before it would have been everlasting too late, since he was acting out of ignorance and immaturity. This is how God's grace works!

All this I say, in His presence, and with Brotherly love. Amen.

# REFERENCES

*New International Version*. Biblica, 2011. Biblegateway.com, https:// www.biblegateway.com.

Schnieders, PC. (2012). *The Books of Enoch: Complete Edition*. (1st ed.). International Alliance Pro-Publishing, LLC. Las Vegas, Nevada.

Identity Network. *Kim Clement: In 2006, God Says ...* Online @:

http://65583.stablerack.com/apps/articles/default.asp?blogid= 2093&view=post&articleid=16858&link=1&fldKeywords=&fld Author=&fldTopic=0.

YouTube. *Crime and Punishment* (Dr. JW, 2021). Online at:

https://www.youtube.com/watch?v=439K_fYVSJM.

Printed in the United States
by Baker & Taylor Publisher Services